ANSWER TO JOB

from
The Collected Works of C. G. Jung
VOLUME 11
BOLLINGEN SERIES XX

ANSWER TO
JOB

C. G. JUNG

TRANSLATED BY R. F. C. HULL

BOLLINGEN SERIES

PRINCETON UNIVERSITY PRESS

First Princeton/Bollingen Paperback Edition, 1973
Ninth Printing, 1991

Extracted from *Psychology and Religion: West and East,* Vol. 11 of
the *Collected Works of C. G. Jung.* All the volumes comprising the
Collected Works constitute number XX in Bollingen Series, under
the editorship of Herbert Read (d. 1968), Michael Fordham, and
Gerhard Adler; executive editor, William McGuire.

"Answer to Job," as it appeared in the first edition of *Psychology
and Religion: West and East,* was published in a Meridian Books
paperback edition (New York, 1960).

15 14 13 12 11 10 9

LIBRARY OF CONGRESS CATALOGUE CARD NUMBER: 72-6097
ISBN 0-691-01785-9
MANUFACTURED IN THE U.S.A.

EDITORIAL NOTE

Answer to Job occupies a unique place in Jung's writings. It is the most intimate and at the same time the most controversial book he has ever written. Without claiming rigid scientific status it contains the most profound insights born out of an intense feeling of inner obligation. Thus Jung wrote to a correspondent that "the motive for my book was an increasingly urgent feeling of responsibility which in the end I could no longer withstand" (letter to Walther Uhsadel, 6 Feb. 1952).[1] He was fully aware of the controversial character of his ideas and of the hostility it was bound to awaken. For a long time he had resisted writing the book, being conscious of the *petra scandali* it would be to many people, even those who had been receptive to his unorthodox views. But in writing it he felt himself the instrument of a higher power: "If there is anything like the spirit seizing one by the scruff of the neck, it is the way this book came into being" (letter to Aniela Jaffé, 18 July 1951).

At the same time the book was a highly personal and emotional argument through which Jung tried to formulate his answer to the questions of evil and the ambiguity of the divine image, with its bright and dark side—problems which had occupied his mind for a lifetime. In a sense the book is an attempt, from intense personal experience, to make his peace with this ambivalent God who could allow his faithful servant Job to become the object of a wager with Satan and permit the untold suffering of millions in Jung's own time. In a letter to H. Schär of 16 Nov. 1951 he wrote: "I had to wrench myself free of God, so to speak, in order to find that unity in myself which God seeks through man. It is rather like that vision of Symeon the Theolo-

1 From *C. G. Jung: Letters*, selected and edited by Gerhard Adler in collaboration with Aniela Jaffé (2 vols., Princeton and London, 1973–74); also the two following quotations.

gian, who sought God in vain everywhere in the world, until God rose like a little sun in his own heart."

It is from this aspect of profound responsibility and intimate searching for truth that the book has to be understood; reading it with this awareness will reveal its full significance.

June 1972   GERHARD ADLER

*

Antwort auf Hiob was originally published in Zurich in 1952, Jung's 77th year. R. F. C. Hull's translation was first published in London in 1954, and two years later by the Pastoral Psychology Book Club in the United States. For the Club's journal, *Pastoral Psychology,* Jung wrote an account of the publication of the book, and this was printed as a prefatory note when the work was taken into Vol. 11 of the Collected Works (1958).[2] A paperback edition was issued by Meridian Books in 1960.

Mr. Hull acknowledged his thanks to Dr. James Kirsch, of Los Angeles, for making available to him his private translation of *Answer to Job* and for his helpful criticism during personal discussions. Professor Jung read the Hull translation in proof and "was kind enough to clarify certain controversial points with unfailing patience and good humour."

---

[2] The prefatory note was originally written as a letter (in English) to Simon Doniger, editor of *Pastoral Psychology,* in November 1955. It was discovered during the editing of the *Letters* that an important phrase had been omitted in the note as published. This omission has now been restored; the second sentence of the fourth paragraph therefore reads: "The crucial question of πόθεν τὸ κακόν (whence evil?) forms the point of departure for the Christian theory of Redemption."

TABLE OF CONTENTS

PREFATORY NOTE [1]

The suggestion that I should tell you how *Answer to Job* came to be written sets me a difficult task, because the history of this book can hardly be told in a few words. I have been occupied with its central problem for years. Many different sources nourished the stream of its thoughts, until one day—and after long reflection—the time was ripe to put them into words.

The most immediate cause of my writing the book is perhaps to be found in certain problems discussed in my book *Aion,* especially the problems of Christ as a symbolic figure and of the antagonism Christ-Antichrist, represented in the traditional zodiacal symbolism of the two fishes.

In connection with the discussion of these problems and of the doctrine of Redemption, I criticized the idea of the *privatio boni* as not agreeing with the psychological findings. Psychological experience shows that whatever we call "good" is balanced by an equally substantial "bad" or "evil." If "evil" is non-existent, then whatever there is must needs be "good." Dogmatically, neither "good" nor "evil" can be derived from Man, since the "Evil One" existed before Man as one of the "Sons of God." The idea of the *privatio boni* began to play a role in the Church only after Mani. Before this heresy, Clement of Rome taught

1 [Written for *Pastoral Psychology* (Great Neck, N. Y.), VI:60 (January, 1956).— EDITORS.]

that God rules the world with a right and a left hand, the right being Christ, the left Satan. Clement's view is clearly *monotheistic,* as it unites the opposites in one God.

Later Christianity, however, is dualistic, inasmuch as it splits off one half of the opposites, personified in Satan, and he is *eternal* in his state of damnation. This crucial question of πόθεν τὸ κακόν (whence evil?) forms the point of departure for the Christian theory of Redemption. It is therefore of prime importance. If Christianity claims to be a monotheism, it becomes unavoidable to assume the opposites as being contained in God. But then we are confronted with a major religious problem: the problem of Job. It is the aim of my book to point out its historical evolution since the time of Job down through the centuries to the most recent symbolic phenomena, such as the *Assumptio Mariae,* etc.

Moreover, the study of medieval natural philosophy—of the greatest importance to psychology—made me try to find an answer to the question: what image of God did these old philosophers have? Or rather: how should the symbols which supplement their image of God be understood? All this pointed to a *complexio oppositorum* and thus recalled again the story of Job to my mind: Job who expected help from God against God. This most peculiar fact presupposes a similar conception of the opposites in God.

On the other hand, numerous questions, not only from my patients, but from all over the world, brought up the problem of giving a more complete and explicit answer than I had given in *Aion.* For many years I hesitated to do this because I was quite conscious of the probable consequences, and knew what a storm would be raised. But I was gripped by the urgency and difficulty of the problem and was unable to throw it off. Therefore I found myself obliged to deal with the whole problem, and I did so in the form of describing a personal experience, carried by subjective emotions. I deliberately chose this form because I wanted to avoid the impression that I had any idea of announcing an "eternal truth." The book does not pretend to be anything but the voice or question of a single individual who hopes or expects to meet with thoughtfulness in the public.

LECTORI BENEVOLO

I am distressed for thee, my brother . . .
II Samuel 1:26 (AV)

553 On account of its somewhat unusual content, my little book requires a short preface. I beg of you, dear reader, not to overlook it. For, in what follows, I shall speak of the venerable objects of religious belief. Whoever talks of such matters inevitably runs the risk of being torn to pieces by the two parties who are in mortal conflict about those very things. This conflict is due to the strange supposition that a thing is true only if it presents itself as a *physical* fact. Thus some people believe it to be physically true that Christ was born as the son of a virgin, while others deny this as a physical impossibility. Everyone can see that there is no logical solution to this conflict and that one would do better not to get involved in such sterile disputes. Both are right and both are wrong. Yet they could easily reach agreement if only they dropped the word "physical." "Physical" is not the only criterion of truth: there are also *psychic* truths which can neither be explained nor proved nor contested in any physical way. If, for instance, a general belief existed that the river Rhine had at one time flowed backwards from its mouth to its source, then this belief would in itself be a fact even though such an assertion, physically understood, would be

xi

deemed utterly incredible. Beliefs of this kind are psychic facts which cannot be contested and need no proof.

554   Religious statements are of this type. They refer without exception to things that cannot be established as physical facts. If they did not do this, they would inevitably fall into the category of the natural sciences. Taken as referring to anything physical, they make no sense whatever, and science would dismiss them as non-experienceable. They would be mere miracles, which are sufficiently exposed to doubt as it is, and yet they could not demonstrate the reality of the spirit or *meaning* that underlies them, because meaning is something that always demonstrates itself and is experienced on its own merits. The spirit and meaning of Christ are present and perceptible to us even without the aid of miracles. Miracles appeal only to the understanding of those who cannot perceive the meaning. They are mere substitutes for the not understood reality of the spirit. This is not to say that the living presence of the spirit is not occasionally accompanied by marvellous physical happenings. I only wish to emphasize that these happenings can neither replace nor bring about an understanding of the spirit, which is the one essential thing.

555   The fact that religious statements frequently conflict with the observed physical phenomena proves that in contrast to physical perception the spirit is autonomous, and that psychic experience is to a certain extent independent of physical data. The psyche is an autonomous factor, and religious statements are psychic confessions which in the last resort are based on unconscious, i.e., on transcendental, processes. These processes are not accessible to physical perception but demonstrate their existence through the confessions of the psyche. The resultant statements are filtered through the medium of human consciousness: that is to say, they are given visible forms which in their turn are subject to manifold influences from within and without. That is why whenever we speak of religious contents we move in a world of images that point to something ineffable. We do not know how clear or unclear these images, metaphors, and concepts are in respect of their transcendental object. If, for instance, we say "God," we give expression to an image or verbal concept which has undergone many changes in the course of time. We are, however, unable to say with any degree of cer-

tainty—unless it be by faith—whether these changes affect only the images and concepts, or the Unspeakable itself. After all, we can imagine God as an eternally flowing current of vital energy that endlessly changes shape just as easily as we can imagine him as an eternally unmoved, unchangeable essence. Our reason is sure only of one thing: that it manipulates images and ideas which are dependent on human imagination and its temporal and local conditions, and which have therefore changed innumerable times in the course of their long history. There is no doubt that there is something behind these images that transcends consciousness and operates in such a way that the statements do not vary limitlessly and chaotically, but clearly all relate to a few basic principles or archetypes. These, like the psyche itself, or like matter, are unknowable as such. All we can do is to construct models of them which we know to be inadequate, a fact which is confirmed again and again by religious statements.

556   If, therefore, in what follows I concern myself with these "metaphysical" objects, I am quite conscious that I am moving in a world of images and that none of my reflections touches the essence of the Unknowable. I am also too well aware of how limited are our powers of conception—to say nothing of the feebleness and poverty of language—to imagine that my remarks mean anything more in principle than what a primitive man means when he conceives of his god as a hare or a snake. But, although our whole world of religious ideas consists of anthropomorphic images that could never stand up to rational criticism, we should never forget that they are based on numinous archetypes, i.e., on an emotional foundation which is unassailable by reason. We are dealing with psychic facts which logic can overlook but not eliminate. In this connection Tertullian has already appealed, quite rightly, to the testimony of the soul. In his *De testimonio animae,* he says:

These testimonies of the soul are as simple as they are true, as obvious as they are simple, as common as they are obvious, as natural as they are common, as divine as they are natural. I think that they cannot appear to any one to be trifling and ridiculous if he considers the majesty of Nature, whence the authority of the soul is derived. What you allow to the mistress you will assign to the disciple. Nature is the mistress, the soul is the disciple; what the one has taught, or

xiii

the other has learned, has been delivered to them by God, who is, in truth, the Master even òf the mistress herself. What notion the soul is able to conceive of her first teacher is in your power to judge, from that sóul which is in you. Feel that which causes you to feel; think upon that which is in forebodings your prophet; in omens, your augur; in the events which befall you, your foreseer. Strange if, being given by God, she knows how to act the diviner for men! Equally strange if she knows Him by whom she has been given! [1]

557   I would go a step further and say that the statements made in the Holy Scriptures are also utterances of the soul—even at the risk of being suspected of psychologism. The statements of the conscious mind may easily be snares and delusions, lies, or arbitrary opinions, but this is certainly not true of the statements of the soul: to begin with they always go over our heads because they point to realities that transcend consciousness. These *entia* are the archetypes of the collective unconscious, and they precipitate complexes of ideas in the form of mythological motifs. Ideas of this kind are never invented, but enter the field of inner perception as finished products, for instance in dreams. They are spontaneous phenomena which are not subject to our will, and we are therefore justified in ascribing to them a certain autonomy. They are to be regarded not only as objects but as subjects with laws of their own. From the point of view of consciousness, we can, of course, describe them as objects, and even explain them up to a point, in the same measure as we can describe and explain a living human being. But then we have to disregard their autonomy. If that is considered, we are compelled to treat them as subjects; in other words, we have to admit that they possess spontaneity and purposiveness, or a kind of consciousness and free will. We observe their behaviour and consider their statements. This dual standpoint, which we are forced to adopt towards every relatively independent organism, naturally has a dual result. On the one hand it tells me what I do to the object, and on the other hand what it does (possibly to me). It is obvious that this unavoidable dualism will create a certain amount of confusion in the minds of my readers, particularly as in what follows we shall have to do with the archetype of Deity.

[1] Cap. V, in Migne, *P.L.*, vol. 1, cols. 615f. (trans. by C. Dodgson, I, pp. 138f., slightly modified.

558 Should any of my readers feel tempted to add an apologetic "only" to the God-images as we perceive them, he would immediately fall foul of experience, which demonstrates beyond any shadow of doubt the extraordinary numinosity of these images. The tremendous effectiveness (mana) of these images is such that they not only give one the feeling of pointing to the *Ens realissimum,* but make one convinced that they actually express it and establish it as a fact. This makes discussion uncommonly difficult, if not impossible. It is, in fact, impossible to demonstrate God's reality to oneself except by using images which have arisen spontaneously or are sanctified by tradition, and whose psychic nature and effects the naïve-minded person has never separated from their unknowable metaphysical background. He instantly equates the effective image with the transcendental *x* to which it points. The seeming justification for this procedure appears self-evident and is not considered a problem so long as the statements of religion are not seriously questioned. But if there is occasion for criticism, then it must be remembered that the image and the statement are psychic processes which are different from their transcendental object; they do not posit it, they merely point to it. In the realm of psychic processes criticism and discussion are not only permissible but are unavoidable.

559 In what follows I shall attempt just such a discussion, such a "coming to terms" with certain religious traditions and ideas. Since I shall be dealing with numinous factors, my feeling is challenged quite as much as my intellect. I cannot, therefore, write in a coolly objective manner, but must allow my emotional subjectivity to speak if I want to describe what I feel when I read certain books of the Bible, or when I remember the impressions I have received from the doctrines of our faith. I do not write as a biblical scholar (which I am not), but as a layman and physician who has been privileged to see deeply into the psychic life of many people. What I am expressing is first of all my own personal view, but I know that I also speak in the name of many who have had similar experiences.

ANSWER TO JOB

ANSWER TO JOB

560   The Book of Job is a landmark in the long historical development of a divine drama. At the time the book was written,
there were already many testimonies which had given a contradictory picture of Yahweh—the picture of a God who knew no
moderation in his emotions and suffered precisely from this lack
of moderation. He himself admitted that he was eaten up with
rage and jealousy and that this knowledge was painful to him.
Insight existed along with obtuseness, loving-kindness along
with cruelty, creative power along with destructiveness. Everything was there, and none of these qualities was an obstacle to
the other. Such a condition is only conceivable either when no
reflecting consciousness is present at all, or when the capacity
for reflection is very feeble and a more or less adventitious phenomenon. A condition of this sort can only be described as
amoral.

561   How the people of the Old Testament felt about their God
we know from the testimony of the Bible. That is not what I
am concerned with here, but rather with the way in which a
modern man with a Christian education and background comes
to terms with the divine darkness which is unveiled in the Book
of Job, and what effect it has on him. I shall not give a cool and
carefully considered exegesis that tries to be fair to every detail,
but a purely subjective reaction. In this way I hope to act as a

3

voice for many who feel the same way as I do, and to give expression to the shattering emotion which the unvarnished spectacle of divine savagery and ruthlessness produces in us. Even if we know by hearsay about the suffering and discord in the Deity, they are so unconscious, and hence so ineffectual morally, that they arouse no human sympathy or understanding. Instead, they give rise to an equally ill-considered outburst of affect, and a smouldering resentment that may be compared to a slowly healing wound. And just as there is a secret tie between the wound and the weapon, so the affect corresponds to the violence of the deed that caused it.

562   The Book of Job serves as a paradigm for a certain experience of God which has a special significance for us today. These experiences come upon man from inside as well as from outside, and it is useless to interpret them rationalistically and thus weaken them by apotropaic means. It is far better to admit the affect and submit to its violence than to try to escape it by all sorts of intellectual tricks or by emotional value-judgments. Although, by giving way to the affect, one imitates all the bad qualities of the outrageous act that provoked it and thus makes oneself guilty of the same fault, that is precisely the point of the whole proceeding: the violence is meant to penetrate to a man's vitals, and he to succumb to its action. He must be affected by it, otherwise its full effect will not reach him. But he should know, or learn to know, what has affected him, for in this way he transforms the blindness of the violence on the one hand and of the affect on the other into knowledge.

563   For this reason I shall express my affect fearlessly and ruthlessly in what follows, and I shall answer injustice with injustice, that I may learn to know why and to what purpose Job was wounded, and what consequences have grown out of this for Yahweh as well as for man.

4

564   Job answers Yahweh thus:

> Behold, I am of small account; what shall I answer thee?
> I lay my hand on my mouth.
> I have spoken once, and I will not answer;
> twice, but I will proceed no further.[1]

565   And indeed, in the immediate presence of the infinite power of creation, this is the only possible answer for a witness who is still trembling in every limb with the terror of almost total annihilation. What else could a half-crushed human worm, grovelling in the dust, reasonably answer in the circumstances? In spite of his pitiable littleness and feebleness, this man knows that he is confronted with a superhuman being who is personally most easily provoked. He also knows that it is far better to withhold all moral reflections, to say nothing of certain moral requirements which might be expected to apply to a god.

566   Yahweh's "justice" is praised, so presumably Job could bring his complaint and the protestation of his innocence before him as

---

1 Job 40:4-5. [Quotations throughout are from the Revised Standard Version (RSV), except where the Authorized Version (AV) is closer to the text of the Zürcher Bibel (ZB) used by the author in conjunction with the original Hebrew and Greek sources. Where neither RSV nor AV fits, I have translated direct from ZB. The poetic line-arrangement of RSV is followed in so far as possible.—TRANS.]

the just judge. But he doubts this possibility. "How can a man be just before God?" [2] "If I summoned him and he answered me, I would not believe that he was listening to my voice." [3] "If it is a matter of justice, who can summon him?" [4] He "multiplies my wounds without cause." [5] "He destroys both the blameless and the wicked." [6] "If the scourge slay suddenly, he will laugh at the trial of the innocent." [7] "I know," Job says to Yahweh, "thou wilt not hold me innocent. I shall be condemned." [8] "If I wash myself . . . never so clean, yet shalt thou plunge me in the ditch." [9] "For he is not a man, as I am, that I should answer him, and we should come together in judgment." [10] Job wants to explain his point of view to Yahweh, to state his complaint, and tells him: "Thou knowest that I am not guilty, and there is none to deliver out of thy hand." [11] "I desire to argue my case with God." [12] "I will defend my ways to his face," [13] "I know that I shall be vindicated." [14] Yahweh should summon him and render him an account or at least allow him to plead his cause. Properly estimating the disproportion between man and God, he asks: "Wilt thou break a leaf driven to and fro? and wilt thou pursue the dry stubble?" [15] God has put him in the wrong, but there is no justice.[16] He has "taken away my right." [17] "Till I die I will not put away my integrity from me. I hold fast to my righteousness, and will not let it go." [18] His friend Elihu the Buzite does not believe the injustice of Yahweh: "Of a truth, God will not do wickedly, and the Almighty will not pervert justice." [19] Illogically enough, he bases his opinion on God's *power*: "Is it fit to say to a king, Thou art wicked? and to princes, Ye are ungodly?" [20] One must "respect the persons of princes and esteem the high more than the low." [21] But Job is not shaken in his faith, and had already uttered an important truth when he said: "Behold, my witness is in heaven, and he that vouches for me is on high . . . my eye pours out tears to God, that he would maintain the right of a man with God, like that of a man with his neighbour." [22] And

---

2 Job 9:2. 3 9:16. 4 9:19. 5 9:17. 6 9:22.
7 9:23 (AV). 8 9:28, 29. 9 9:30–31 (AV). 10 9:32 (AV).
11 10:7. 12 13:3. 13 13:15. 14 13:18. 15 13:25 (AV).
16 19:6–7. 17 27:2. 18 27:5–6. 19 34:12. 20 34:18 (AV).
21 34:19 (ZB). 22 16:19–21.

later: "For I know that my Vindicator lives, and at last he will stand upon the earth." [23]

567　These words clearly show that Job, in spite of his doubt as to whether man can be just before God, still finds it difficult to relinquish the idea of meeting God on the basis of justice and therefore of morality. Because, in spite of everything, he cannot give up his faith in divine justice, it is not easy for him to accept the knowledge that divine arbitrariness breaks the law. On the other hand, he has to admit that no one except Yahweh himself is doing him injustice and violence. He cannot deny that he is up against a God who does not care a rap for any moral opinion and does not recognize any form of ethics as binding. This is perhaps the greatest thing about Job, that, faced with this difficulty, he does not doubt the unity of God. He clearly sees that God is at odds with himself—so totally at odds that he, Job, is quite certain of finding in God a helper and an "advocate" against God. As certain as he is of the evil in Yahweh, he is equally certain of the good. In a human being who renders us evil we cannot expect at the same time to find a helper. But Yahweh is not a human being: he is both a persecutor and a helper in one, and the one aspect is as real as the other. Yahweh is not split but is an *antinomy*—a totality of inner opposites— and this is the indispensable condition for his tremendous dynamism, his omniscience and omnipotence. Because of this knowledge Job holds on to his intention of "defending his ways to his face," i.e., of making his point of view clear to him, since notwithstanding his wrath, Yahweh is also man's advocate *against himself* when man puts forth his complaint.

568　One would be even more astonished at Job's knowledge of God if this were the first time one were hearing of Yahweh's amorality. His incalculable moods and devastating attacks of wrath had, however, been known from time immemorial. He had proved himself to be a jealous defender of morality and was specially sensitive in regard to justice. Hence he had always to be praised as "just," which, it seemed, was very important to him. Thanks to this circumstance or peculiarity of his, he had a *distinct personality*, which differed from that of a more or less archaic king only in scope. His jealous and irritable nature,

23 19:25. ['Vindicator' is RSV alternative reading for 'Redeemer,' and comes very close to the ZB *Anwalt*, 'advocate.'—TRANS.]

prying mistrustfully into the faithless hearts of men and exploring their secret thoughts, compelled a personal relationship between himself and man, who could not help but feel personally called by him. That was the essential difference between Yahweh and the all-ruling Father Zeus, who in a benevolent and somewhat detached manner allowed the economy of the universe to roll along on its accustomed courses and punished only those who were disorderly. He did not moralize but ruled purely instinctively. He did not demand anything more *from* human beings than the sacrifices due to him; he did not want to do anything *with* human beings because he had no plans for them. Father Zeus is certainly a figure but not a personality. Yahweh, on the other hand, was interested in man. Human beings were a matter of first-rate importance to him. He needed them as they needed him, urgently and personally. Zeus too could throw thunderbolts about, but only at hopelessly disorderly individuals. Against mankind as a whole he had no objections—but then they did not interest him all that much. Yahweh, however, could get inordinately excited about man as a species and men as individuals if they did not behave as he desired or expected, without ever considering that in his omnipotence he could easily have created something better than these "bad earthenware pots."

569   In view of this intense personal relatedness to his chosen people, it was only to be expected that a regular covenant would develop which also extended to certain individuals, for instance to David. As we learn from the Eighty-ninth Psalm, Yahweh told him:

> My steadfast love I will keep for him for ever,
> and my covenant will stand firm for him.
>
> .   .   .   .
>
> I will not violate my covenant,
> or alter the word that went forth from my lips.
> Once for all I have sworn by my holiness;
> I will not lie to David.[24]

570   And yet it happened that he, who watched so jealously over the fulfilment of laws and contracts, broke his own oath. Modern man, with his sensitive conscience, would have felt the black

[24] Verses 28, 34, 35.

8

abyss opening and the ground giving way under his feet, for the least he expects of his God is that he should be superior to mortal man in the sense of being better, higher, nobler—but not his superior in the kind of moral flexibility and unreliability that do not jib even at perjury.

571　Of course one must not tax an archaic god with the requirements of modern ethics. For the people of early antiquity things were rather different. In their gods there was absolutely everything: they teemed with virtues and vices. Hence they could be punished, put in chains, deceived, stirred up against one another without losing face, or at least not for long. The man of that epoch was so inured to divine inconsistencies that he was not unduly perturbed when they happened. With Yahweh the case was different because, from quite early on, the personal and moral tie began to play an important part in the religious relationship. In these circumstances a breach of contract was bound to have the effect not only of a personal but of a moral injury. One can see this from the way David answers Yahweh:

> How long, Lord? wilt thou hide thyself for ever?
> 　shall thy wrath burn like fire?
> Remember how short my time is:
> 　wherefore hast thou made all men in vain?
>
> .　.　.　.　.　.　.　.　.　.　.　.　.　.　.
>
> Lord, where are thy former lovingkindnesses,
> 　which by thy faithfulness thou didst swear to David? [25]

572　Had this been addressed to a human being it would have run something like this: "For heaven's sake, man, pull yourself together and stop being such a senseless savage! It is really too grotesque to get into such a rage when it's partly your own fault that the plants won't flourish. You used to be quite reasonable and took good care of the garden you planted, instead of trampling it to pieces."

573　Certainly our interlocutor would never dare to remonstrate with his almighty partner about this breach of contract. He knows only too well what a row he would get into if *he* were the wretched breaker of the law. Because anything else would put him in peril of his life, he must retire to the more exalted plane

[25] Psalm 89:46, 47, 49 (AV; last line from RSV).

9

of reason. In this way, without knowing it or wanting it, he shows himself superior to his divine partner both intellectually and morally. Yahweh fails to notice that he is being humoured, just as little as he understands why he has continually to be praised as just. He makes pressing demands on his people to be praised [26] and propitiated in every possible way, for the obvious purpose of keeping him in a good temper at any price.

574   The character thus revealed fits a personality who can only convince himself that he exists through his relation to an object. Such dependence on the object is absolute when the subject is totally lacking in self-reflection and therefore has no insight into himself. It is as if he existed only by reason of the fact that he has an object which assures him that he is really there. If Yahweh, as we would expect of a sensible human being, were really conscious of himself, he would, in view of the true facts of the case, at least have put an end to the panegyrics on his justice. But he is too unconscious to be moral. Morality presupposes consciousness. By this I do not mean to say that Yahweh is imperfect or evil, like a gnostic demiurge. He is everything in its totality; therefore, among other things, he is total justice, and also its total opposite. At least this is the way he must be conceived if one is to form a unified picture of his character. We must only remember that what we have sketched is no more than an anthropomorphic picture which is not even particularly easy to visualize. From the way the divine nature expresses itself we can see that the individual qualities are not adequately related to one another, with the result that they fall apart into mutually contradictory acts. For instance, Yahweh regrets having created human beings, although in his omniscience he must have known all along what would happen to them.

II

575   Since the Omniscient looks into all hearts, and Yahweh's eyes "run to and fro through the whole earth," [1] it were better for the interlocutor of the Eighty-ninth Psalm not to wax

---

[26] Or to be "blessed," which is even more captious of him.

[1] Zechariah 4: 10 (AV). Cf. also the Wisdom of Solomon 1: 10 (AV): "For the ear of jealousy heareth all things: and the noise of murmurings is not hid."

too conscious of his slight moral superiority over the more unconscious God. Better to keep it dark, for Yahweh is no friend of critical thoughts which in any way diminish the tribute of recognition he demands. Loudly as his power resounds through the universe, the basis of its existence is correspondingly slender, for it needs conscious reflection in order to exist in reality. Existence is only real when it is conscious to somebody. That is why the Creator needs conscious man even though, from sheer unconsciousness, he would like to prevent him from becoming conscious. And that is also why Yahweh needs the acclamation of a small group of people. One can imagine what would happen if this assembly suddenly decided to stop the applause: there would be a state of high excitation, with outbursts of blind destructive rage, then a withdrawal into hellish loneliness and the torture of non-existence, followed by a gradual reawakening of an unutterable longing for something which would make him conscious of himself. It is probably for this reason that all pristine things, even man before he becomes the canaille, have a touching, magical beauty, for in its nascent state "each thing after its kind" is the most precious, the most desirable, the tenderest thing in the world, being a reflection of the infinite love and goodness of the Creator.

576   In view of the undoubted frightfulness of divine wrath, and in an age when men still knew what they were talking about when they said "Fear God," it was only to be expected that man's slight superiority should have remained unconscious. The powerful personality of Yahweh, who, in addition to everything else, lacked all biographical antecedents (his original relationship to the Elohim had long since been sunk in oblivion), had raised him above all the numina of the Gentiles and had immunized him against the influence that for several centuries had been undermining the authority of the pagan gods. It was precisely the details of their mythological biography that had become their nemesis, for with his growing capacity for judgment man had found these stories more and more incomprehensible and indecent. Yahweh, however, had no origin and no past, except his creation of the world, with which all history began, and his relation to that part of mankind whose forefather Adam he had fashioned in his own image as the Anthropos, the original man, by what appears to have been a special act of creation.

11

One can only suppose that the other human beings who must also have existed at that time had been formed previously on the divine potter's wheel along with the various kinds of beasts and cattle—those human beings, namely, from whom Cain and Seth chose their wives. If one does not approve of this conjecture, then the only other possibility that remains is the far more scandalous one that they incestuously married their sisters (for whom there is no evidence in the text), as was still surmised by the philosopher Karl Lamprecht at the end of the nineteenth century.

577   The special providence which singled out the Jews from among the divinely stamped portion of humanity and made them the "chosen people" had burdened them from the start with a heavy obligation. As usually happens with such mortgages, they quite understandably tried to circumvent it as much as possible. Since the chosen people used every opportunity to break away from him, and Yahweh felt it of vital importance to tie this indispensable object (which he had made "godlike" for this very purpose) definitely to himself, he proposed to the patriarch Noah a contract between himself on the one hand, and Noah, his children, and all their animals, both tame and wild, on the other—a contract that promised advantages to both parties. In order to strengthen this contract and keep it fresh in the memory, he instituted the rainbow as a token of the covenant. If, in future, he summoned the thunder-clouds which hide within them floods of water and lightning, then the rainbow would appear, reminding him and his people of the contract. The temptation to use such an accumulation of clouds for an experimental deluge was no small one, and it was therefore a good idea to associate it with a sign that would give timely warning of possible catastrophe.

578   In spite of these precautions the contract had gone to pieces with David, an event which left behind it a literary deposit in the Scriptures and which grieved some few of the devout, who upon reading it became reflective. As the Psalms were zealously read, it was inevitable that certain thoughtful people were unable to stomach the Eighty-ninth Psalm. However that may be, the fatal impression made by the breach of contract survived.[2]

[2] The 89th Psalm is attributed to David and is supposed to have been a community song written in exile.

It is historically possible that these considerations influenced the author of the Book of Job.

579   The Book of Job places this pious and faithful man, so heavily afflicted by the Lord, on a brightly lit stage where he presents his case to the eyes and ears of the world. It is amazing to see how easily Yahweh, quite without reason, had let himself be influenced by one of his sons, by a *doubting thought*,[3] and made unsure of Job's faithfulness. With his touchiness and suspiciousness the mere possibility of doubt was enough to infuriate him and induce that peculiar double-faced behaviour of which he had already given proof in the Garden of Eden, when he pointed out the tree to the First Parents and at the same time forbade them to eat of it. In this way he precipitated the Fall, which he apparently never intended. Similarly, his faithful servant Job is now to be exposed to a rigorous moral test, quite gratuitously and to no purpose, although Yahweh is convinced of Job's faithfulness and constancy, and could moreover have assured himself beyond all doubt on this point had he taken counsel with his own omniscience. Why, then, is the experiment made at all, and a bet with the unscrupulous slanderer settled, without a stake, on the back of a powerless creature? It is indeed no edifying spectacle to see how quickly Yahweh abandons his faithful servant to the evil spirit and lets him fall without compunction or pity into the abyss of physical and moral suffering. From the human point of view Yahweh's behaviour is so revolting that one has to ask oneself whether there is not a deeper motive hidden behind it. Has Yahweh some secret resistance against Job? That would explain his yielding to Satan. But what does man possess that God does not have? Because of his littleness, puniness, and defencelessness against the Almighty, he possesses, as we have already suggested, a somewhat keener consciousness based on self-reflection: he must, in order to survive, always be mindful of his impotence. God has no need of this circumspection, for nowhere does he come up against an insuperable obstacle that would force him to hesitate and hence make him reflect on himself. Could a suspicion have grown up in God that man possesses an infinitely small yet more concentrated

---

3 Satan is presumably one of God's eyes which "go to and fro in the earth and walk up and down in it" (Job 1:7). In Persian tradition, Ahriman proceeded from one of Ormuzd's doubting thoughts.

light than he, Yahweh, possesses? A jealousy of that kind might perhaps explain his behaviour. It would be quite explicable if some such dim, barely understood deviation from the definition of a mere "creature" had aroused his divine suspicions. Too often already these human beings had not behaved in the pre-scribed manner. Even his trusty servant Job might have some-thing up his sleeve. . . . Hence Yahweh's surprising readiness to listen to Satan's insinuations against his better judgment.

580   Without further ado Job is robbed of his herds, his servants are slaughtered, his sons and daughters are killed by a whirl-wind, and he himself is smitten with sickness and brought to the brink of the grave. To rob him of peace altogether, his wife and his old friends are let loose against him, all of whom say the wrong things. His justified complaint finds no hearing with the judge who is so much praised for his justice. Job's right is refused in order that Satan be not disturbed in his play.

581   One must bear in mind here the dark deeds that follow one another in quick succession: robbery, murder, bodily injury with premeditation, and denial of a fair trial. This is further exacerbated by the fact that Yahweh displays no compunction, remorse, or compassion, but only ruthlessness and brutality. The plea of unconsciousness is invalid, seeing that he flagrantly violates at least three of the commandments he himself gave out on Mount Sinai.

582   Job's friends do everything in their power to contribute to his moral torments, and instead of giving him, whom God has perfidiously abandoned, their warm-hearted support, they mor-alize in an all too human manner, that is, in the stupidest fash-ion imaginable, and "fill him with wrinkles." They thus deny him even the last comfort of sympathetic participation and human understanding, so that one cannot altogether suppress the suspicion of connivance in high places.

583   Why Job's torments and the divine wager should suddenly come to an end is not quite clear. So long as Job does not actu-ally die, the pointless suffering could be continued indefinitely. We must, however, keep an eye on the background of all these events: it is just possible that something in this background will gradually begin to take shape as a compensation for Job's un-deserved suffering—something to which Yahweh, even if he had only a faint inkling of it, could hardly remain indifferent. With-

out Yahweh's knowledge and contrary to his intentions, the tormented though guiltless Job had secretly been lifted up to a superior knowledge of God which God himself did not possess. Had Yahweh consulted his omniscience, Job would not have had the advantage of him. But then, so many other things would not have happened either.

584   Job realizes God's inner antinomy, and in the light of this realization his knowledge attains a divine numinosity. The possibility of this development lies, one must suppose, in man's "godlikeness," which one should certainly not look for in human morphology. Yahweh himself had guarded against this error by expressly forbidding the making of images. Job, by his insistence on bringing his case before God, even without hope of a hearing, had stood his ground and thus created the very obstacle that forced God to reveal his true nature. With this dramatic climax Yahweh abruptly breaks off his cruel game of cat and mouse. But if anyone should expect that his wrath will now be turned against the slanderer, he will be severely disappointed. Yahweh does not think of bringing this mischief-making son of his to account, nor does it ever occur to him to give Job at least the moral satisfaction of explaining his behaviour. Instead, he comes riding along on the tempest of his almightiness and thunders reproaches at the half-crushed human worm:

> Who is this that darkens counsel
> by words without insight? [4]

585   In view of the subsequent words of Yahweh, one must really ask oneself: *Who* is darkening *what* counsel? The only dark thing here is how Yahweh ever came to make a bet with Satan. It is certainly not Job who has darkened anything and least of all a counsel, for there was never any talk of this nor will there be in what follows. The bet does not contain any "counsel" so far as one can see—unless, of course, it was Yahweh himself who egged Satan on for the ultimate purpose of exalting Job. Naturally this development was foreseen in omniscience, and it may be that the word "counsel" refers to this eternal and absolute knowledge. If so, Yahweh's attitude seems the more illogical and incomprehensible, as he could then have enlightened Job on this point—which, in view of the wrong done to him, would

4 Job 38: 2 (ZB).

have been only fair and equitable. I must therefore regard this possibility as improbable.

586   *Whose* words are without insight? Presumably Yahweh is not referring to the words of Job's friends, but is rebuking Job. But what is Job's guilt? The only thing he can be blamed for is his incurable optimism in believing that he can appeal to divine justice. In this he is mistaken, as Yahweh's subsequent words prove. God does not want to be just; he merely flaunts might over right. Job could not get that into his head, because he looked upon God as a moral being. He had never doubted God's might, but had hoped for right as well. He had, however, already taken back this error when he recognized God's contradictory nature, and by so doing he assigned a place to God's justice and goodness. So one can hardly speak of lack of insight.

587   The answer to Yahweh's conundrum is therefore: it is Yahweh himself who darkens his own counsel and who has no insight. He turns the tables on Job and blames him for what he himself does: man is not permitted to have an opinion about him, and, in particular, is to have no insight which he himself does not possess. For seventy-one verses he proclaims his world-creating power to his miserable victim, who sits in ashes and scratches his sores with potsherds, and who by now has had more than enough of superhuman violence. Job has absolutely no need of being impressed by further exhibitions of this power. Yahweh, in his omniscience, could have known just how incongruous his attempts at intimidation were in such a situation. He could easily have seen that Job believes in his omnipotence as much as ever and has never doubted it or wavered in his loyalty. Altogether, he pays so little attention to Job's real situation that one suspects him of having an ulterior motive which is more important to him: Job is no more than the outward occasion for an inward process of dialectic in God. His thunderings at Job so completely miss the point that one cannot help but see how much he is occupied with himself. The tremendous emphasis he lays on his omnipotence and greatness makes no sense in relation to Job, who certainly needs no more convincing, but only becomes intelligible when aimed at a listener *who doubts it.* This "doubting thought" is Satan, who after completing his evil handiwork has returned to the paternal bosom in order to continue his subversive activity there. Yahweh must have seen

that Job's loyalty was unshakable and that Satan had lost his bet. He must also have realized that, in accepting this bet, he had done everything possible to drive his faithful servant to disloyalty, even to the extent of perpetrating a whole series of crimes. Yet it is not remorse and certainly not moral horror that rises to his consciousness, but an obscure intimation of something that questions his omnipotence. He is particularly sensitive on this point, because "might" is the great argument. But omniscience knows that might excuses nothing. The said intimation refers, of course, to the extremely uncomfortable fact that Yahweh had let himself be bamboozled by Satan. This weakness of his does not reach full consciousness, since Satan is treated with remarkable tolerance and consideration. Evidently Satan's intrigue is deliberately overlooked at Job's expense.

588 Luckily enough, Job had noticed during this harangue that everything else had been mentioned except his right. He has understood that it is at present impossible to argue the question of right, as it is only too obvious that Yahweh has no interest whatever in Job's cause but is far more preoccupied with his own affairs. Satan, that is to say, has somehow to disappear, and this can best be done by casting suspicion on Job as a man of subversive opinions. The problem is thus switched on to another track, and the episode with Satan remains unmentioned and unconscious. To the spectator it is not quite clear why Job is treated to this almighty exhibition of thunder and lightning, but the performance as such is sufficiently magnificent and impressive to convince not only a larger audience but above all Yahweh himself of his unassailable power. Whether Job realizes what violence Yahweh is doing to his own omniscience by behaving like this we do not know, but his silence and submission leave a number of possibilities open. Job has no alternative but formally to revoke his demand for justice, and he therefore answers in the words quoted at the beginning: "I lay my hand on my mouth."

589 He betrays not the slightest trace of mental reservation—in fact, his answer leaves us in no doubt that he has succumbed completely and without question to the tremendous force of the divine demonstration. The most exacting tyrant should have been satisfied with this, and could be quite sure that his servant —from terror alone, to say nothing of his undoubted loyalty—

17

would not dare to nourish a single improper thought for a very long time to come.

590   Strangely enough, Yahweh does not notice anything of the kind. He does not see Job and his situation at all. It is rather as if he had another powerful opponent in the place of Job, one who was better worth challenging. This is clear from his twice-repeated taunt:

> Gird up your loins like a man;
> I will question you, and you shall declare to me.[5]

591   One would have to choose positively grotesque examples to illustrate the disproportion between the two antagonists. Yahweh sees something in Job which we would not ascribe to him but to God, that is, an equal power which causes him to bring out his whole power apparatus and parade it before his opponent. Yahweh projects on to Job a sceptic's face which is hateful to him because it is his own, and which gazes at him with an uncanny and critical eye. He is afraid of it, for only in face of something frightening does one let off a cannonade of references to one's power, cleverness, courage, invincibility, etc. What has all that to do with Job? Is it worth the lion's while to terrify a mouse?

592   Yahweh cannot rest satisfied with the first victorious round. Job has long since been knocked out, but the great antagonist whose phantom is projected on to the pitiable sufferer still stands menacingly upright. Therefore Yahweh raises his arm again:

> Will you even put me in the wrong?
> Will you condemn me that you may be justified?
> Have you an arm like God,
> and can you thunder with a voice like his?[6]

593   Man, abandoned without protection and stripped of his rights, and whose nothingness is thrown in his face at every opportunity, evidently appears to be so dangerous to Yahweh that he must be battered down with the heaviest artillery. What irritates Yahweh can be seen from his challenge to the ostensible Job:

5 Job 38:3 and 40:7.   6 40:8–9.

18

> Look on every one that is proud, and bring him low;
>   and tread down the wicked where they stand.
> Hide them in the dust together;
>   bind their faces in the hidden place.
> Then will I also acknowledge to you
>   that your own right hand can give you victory.[7]

594   Job is challenged as though he himself were a god. But in the contemporary metaphysics there was no *deuteros theos*, no other god except Satan, who owns Yahweh's ear and is able to influence him. He is the only one who can pull the wool over his eyes, beguile him, and put him up to a massive violation of his own penal code. A formidable opponent indeed, and, because of his close kinship, so compromising that he must be concealed with the utmost discretion—even to the point of God's hiding him from his own consciousness in his own bosom! In his stead God must set up his miserable servant as the bugbear whom he has to fight, in the hope that by banishing the dreaded countenance to "the hidden place" he will be able to maintain himself in a state of unconsciousness.

595   The stage-managing of this imaginary duel, the speechifying, and the impressive performance given by the prehistoric menagerie would not be sufficiently explained if we tried to reduce them to the purely negative factor of Yahweh's fear of becoming conscious and of the relativization which this entails. The conflict becomes acute for Yahweh as a result of a new factor, which is, however, not hidden from omniscience—though in this case the existing knowledge is not accompanied by any conclusion. The new factor is something that has never occurred before in the history of the world, the unheard-of fact that, without knowing it or wanting it, a mortal man is raised by his moral behaviour above the stars in heaven, from which position of advantage he can behold the back of Yahweh, the abysmal world of "shards." [8]

---

[7] 40:12–14 ("in the hidden place" is RSV alternative reading for "in the world below").

[8] This is an allusion to an idea found in the later cabalistic philosophy. [These "shards," also called "shells" (Heb. *kelipot*), form ten counterpoles to the ten *sefiroth*, which are the ten stages in the revelation of God's creative power. The shards, representing the forces of evil and darkness, were originally mixed with the light of the *sefiroth*. The *Zohar* describes evil as the by-product of the life

596   Does Job know what he has seen? If he does, he is astute or canny enough not to betray it. But his words speak volumes:

> I know that thou canst do all things,
>   and that no purpose of thine can be thwarted.[9]

597   Truly, Yahweh can do all things and permits himself all things without batting an eyelid. With brazen countenance he can project his shadow side and remain unconscious at man's expense. He can boast of his superior power and enact laws which mean less than air to him. Murder and manslaughter are mere bagatelles, and if the mood takes him he can play the feudal grand seigneur and generously recompense his bondslave for the havoc wrought in his wheat-fields. "So you have lost your sons and daughters? No harm done, I will give you new and better ones."

598   Job continues (no doubt with downcast eyes and in a low voice):

> "Who is this that hides counsel without insight?"
> Therefore I have uttered what I did not understand,
>   things too wonderful for me, which I did not know.
> "Hear, and I will speak;
>   I will question you, and you declare to me."
> I had heard of thee by the hearing of the ear,
>   but now my eye sees thee;
> therefore I abhor myself,
>   and repent in dust and ashes.[10]

599   Shrewdly, Job takes up Yahweh's aggressive words and prostrates himself at his feet as if he were indeed the defeated antagonist. Guileless as Job's speech sounds, it could just as well be equivocal. He has learnt his lesson well and experienced "wonderful things" which are none too easily grasped. Before, he had known Yahweh "by the hearing of the ear," but now he has got a taste of his reality, more so even than David—an

---

process of the *sefiroth*. Therefore the *sefiroth* had to be cleansed of the evil admixture of the shards. This elimination of the shards took place in what is described in the cabalistic writings—particularly of Luria and his school—as the "breaking of the vessels." Through this the powers of evil assumed a separate and real existence. Cf. Scholem, *Major Trends in Jewish Mysticism*, p. 267.—Editors.]   [9] 42:2.   [10] 42:3–6 (modified).

incisive lesson that had better not be forgotten. Formerly he was naïve, dreaming perhaps of a "good" God, or of a benevolent ruler and just judge. He had imagined that a "covenant" was a legal matter and that anyone who was party to a contract could insist on his rights as agreed; that God would be faithful and true or at least just, and, as one could assume from the Ten Commandments, would have some recognition of ethical values or at least feel committed to his own legal standpoint. But, to his horror, he has discovered that Yahweh is not human but, in certain respects, less than human, that he is just what Yahweh himself says of Leviathan (the crocodile):

> He beholds everything that is high:
> He is king over all proud beasts.[11]

600   Unconsciousness has an animal nature. Like all old gods Yahweh has his animal symbolism with its unmistakable borrowings from the much older theriomorphic gods of Egypt, especially Horus and his four sons. Of the four animals of Yahweh only one has a human face. That is probably Satan, the godfather of man as a spiritual being. Ezekiel's vision attributes three-fourths animal nature and only one-fourth human nature to the animal deity, while the upper deity, the one above the "sapphire throne," merely had the "likeness" of a man.[12] This symbolism explains Yahweh's behaviour, which, from the human point of view, is so intolerable: it is the behaviour of an unconscious being who cannot be judged morally. Yahweh is a *phenomenon* and, as Job says, "not a man." [13]

601   One could, without too much difficulty, impute such a meaning to Job's speech. Be that as it may, Yahweh calmed down at last. The therapeutic measure of unresisting acceptance had proved its value yet again. Nevertheless, Yahweh is still some-

---

11 Job 41 : 25 (ZB); cf. 41 : 34 (AV and RSV).   12 Ezekiel 1 : 26.

13 The naïve assumption that the creator of the world is a conscious being must be regarded as a disastrous prejudice which later gave rise to the most incredible dislocations of logic. For example, the nonsensical doctrine of the *privatio boni* would never have been necessary had one not had to assume in advance that it is impossible for the consciousness of a good God to produce evil deeds. Divine unconsciousness and lack of reflection, on the other hand, enable us to form a conception of God which puts his actions beyond moral judgment and allows no conflict to arise between goodness and beastliness.

nervous of Job's friends—they "have not spoken of me what [is] right." [14] The projection of his doubt-complex extends—[logi]cally enough, one must say—to these respectable and slightly pedantic old gentlemen, as though God-knows-what depended on what they thought. But the fact that men should think at all, and especially about him, is maddeningly disquieting and ought somehow to be stopped. It is far too much like the sort of thing his vagrant son is always springing on him, thus hitting him in his weakest spot. How often already has he bitterly regretted his unconsidered outbursts!

602   One can hardly avoid the impression that Omniscience is gradually drawing near to a realization, and is threatened with an insight that seems to be hedged about with fears of self-destruction. Fortunately, Job's final declaration is so formulated that one can assume with some certainty that, for the protagonists, the incident is closed for good and all.

603   We, the commenting chorus on this great tragedy, which has never at any time lost its vitality, do not feel quite like that. For our modern sensibilities it is by no means apparent that with Job's profound obeisance to the majesty of the divine presence, and his prudent silence, a real answer has been given to the question raised by the Satanic prank of a wager with God. Job has not so much answered as reacted in an adjusted way. In so doing he displayed remarkable self-discipline, but an unequivocal answer has still to be given.

604   To take the most obvious thing, what about the moral wrong Job has suffered? Is man so worthless in God's eyes that not even a *tort moral* can be inflicted on him? That contradicts the fact that man is desired by Yahweh and that it obviously matters to him whether men speak "right" of him or not. He needs Job's loyalty, and it means so much to him that he shrinks at nothing in carrying out his test. This attitude attaches an almost divine importance to man, for what else is there in the whole wide world that could mean anything to one who has everything? Yahweh's divided attitude, which on the one hand tramples on human life and happiness without regard, and on the other hand must have man for a partner, puts the latter in an impossible position. At one moment Yahweh behaves as irrationally as a cataclysm; the next moment he wants to be loved, honoured,

14 Job 42:7.

THIS IS, OF COURSE, 22 THE KEY TO IT, MAN MUST HAVE THE OPTION OF CHOOSING (OR NOT CHOOSING) GOD — HENCE, THE NECESSITY OF EVIL, AS WELL AS THE PROOF OF FREE WILL

worshipped, and praised as just. He reacts irritably to every word that has the faintest suggestion of criticism, while he himself does not care a straw for his own moral code if his actions happen to run counter to its statutes.

605 One can submit to such a God only with fear and trembling, and can try indirectly to propitiate the despot with unctuous praises and ostentatious obedience. But a relationship of trust seems completely out of the question to our modern way of thinking. Nor can moral satisfaction be expected from an unconscious nature god of this kind. Nevertheless, Job got his satisfaction, without Yahweh's intending it and possibly without himself knowing it, as the poet would have it appear. Yahweh's allocutions have the unthinking yet none the less transparent purpose of showing Job the brutal power of the demiurge: "This is I, the creator of all the ungovernable, ruthless forces of Nature, which are not subject to any ethical laws. I, too, am an amoral force of Nature, a purely phenomenal personality that cannot see its own back."

606 This is, or at any rate could be, a moral satisfaction of the first order for Job, because through this declaration man, in spite of his impotence, is set up as a judge over God himself. We do not know whether Job realizes this, but we do know from the numerous commentaries on Job that all succeeding ages have overlooked the fact that a kind of Moira or Dike rules over Yahweh, causing him to give himself away so blatantly. Anyone can see how he unwittingly raises Job by humiliating him in the dust. By so doing he pronounces judgment on himself and gives man the moral satisfaction whose absence we found so painful in the Book of Job.

607 The poet of this drama showed a masterly discretion in ringing down the curtain at the very moment when his hero gave unqualified recognition to the ἀπόφασις μεγάλη of the Demiurge by prostrating himself at the feet of His Divine Majesty. No other impression was permitted to remain. An unusual scandal was blowing up in the realm of metaphysics, with supposedly devastating consequences, and nobody was ready with a saving formula which would rescue the monotheistic conception of God from disaster. Even in those days the critical intellect of a Greek could easily have seized on this new addition to Yahweh's biography and used it in his disfavour (as indeed happened,

though very much later) [15] so as to mete out to him the fate that had already overtaken the Greek gods. But a relativization of God was utterly unthinkable at that time, and remained so for the next two thousand years.

608 The unconscious mind of man sees correctly even when conscious reason is blind and impotent. The drama has been consummated for all eternity: Yahweh's dual nature has been revealed, and somebody or something has seen and registered this fact. Such a revelation, whether it reached man's consciousness or not, could not fail to have far-reaching consequences.

III

609 Before turning to the question of how the germ of unrest developed further, we must turn back to the time when the Book of Job was written. Unfortunately the dating is uncertain. It is generally assumed that it was written between 600 and 300 b.c.—not too far away, therefore, from the time of the Book of Proverbs (4th to 3rd century). Now in Proverbs we encounter a symptom of Greek influence which, if an earlier date is assigned to it, reached the Jewish sphere of culture through Asia Minor and, if a later date, through Alexandria. This is the idea of Sophia, or the *Sapientia Dei,* who is a coeternal and more or less hypostatized pneuma of feminine nature that existed before the Creation:

> The Lord possessed me in the beginning of his way,
> before his works of old.
> I was set up from everlasting, from the beginning,
> or ever the earth was.
> When there were no depths, I was brought forth;
> when there were no fountains abounding with water.
>
> .   .   .   .
>
> When he established the heavens, I was there,
>
> .   .   .   .
>
> when he marked out the foundations of the earth,
> then I was by him, as a master workman,

[15] [Cf. Gnostic interpretation of Yahweh as Saturn-Ialdabaoth in "Transformation Symbolism in the Mass," par. 350; *Aion,* par. 128.—EDITORS.]

and I was daily his delight,
    rejoicing always before him,
rejoicing in his habitable earth;
    and my delights were with the sons of men.[1]

610   This Sophia, who already shares certain essential qualities
with the Johannine Logos, is on the one hand closely associated
with the Hebrew Chochma, but on the other hand goes so far
beyond it that one can hardly fail to think of the Indian Shakti.
Relations with India certainly existed at that time (the time of
the Ptolemys). A further source is the Wisdom of Jesus the Son
of Sirach, or Ecclesiasticus, written around 200 B.C. Here Wisdom says of herself:

I came out of the mouth of the most High,
    and covered the earth as a cloud.
I dwelt in high places,
    and my throne is in a cloudy pillar.
I alone encompassed the circuit of heaven,
    and walked in the bottom of the deep.
I had power over the waves of the sea, and over all the
        earth,
    and over every people and nation.

    .   .   .   .

He created me from the beginning before the world,
    and I shall never fail.
In the holy tabernacle I served before him;
    and so was I established in Sion.
Likewise in the beloved city he gave me rest,
    and in Jerusalem was my power.

    .   .   .   .

I was exalted like a cedar in Libanus,
    and as a cypress tree upon the mountains of Hermon.
I was exalted like a palm tree in En-gaddi,
    and as a rose plant in Jericho,
    as a fair olive tree in a pleasant field,
    and grew up as a plane tree by the water.
I gave a sweet smell like cinnamon and aspalathus,
    and I yielded a pleasant odour like the best myrrh . . .
As the turpentine tree I stretched out my branches,
    and my branches are the branches of honour and grace.

1 Proverbs 8:22–24 (AV), 27, 29–31 (AV mod.).

As the vine brought I forth pleasant savour,
    and my flowers are the fruit of honour and riches.
I am the mother of fair love,
    and fear, and knowledge, and holy hope:
    I therefore, being eternal, am given to all my children
    which are chosen of him.[2]

611   It is worth while to examine this text more closely. Wisdom describes herself, in effect, as the Logos, the Word of God ("I came out of the mouth of the most High"). As Ruach, the spirit of God, she brooded over the waters of the beginning. Like God, she has her throne in heaven. As the cosmogonic Pneuma she pervades heaven and earth and all created things. She corresponds in almost every feature to the Logos of St. John. We shall see below how far this connection is also important as regards content.

612   She is the feminine numen of the "metropolis" par excellence, of Jerusalem the mother-city. She is the mother-beloved, a reflection of Ishtar, the pagan city-goddess. This is confirmed by the detailed comparison of Wisdom with trees, such as the cedar, palm, terebinth ("turpentine-tree"), olive, cypress, etc. All these trees have from ancient times been symbols of the Semitic love- and mother-goddess. A holy tree always stood beside her altar on high places. In the Old Testament oaks and terebinths are oracle trees. God or angels are said to appear in or beside trees. David consulted a mulberry-tree oracle.[3] The tree in Babylon represented Tammuz, the son-lover, just as it represented Osiris, Adonis, Attis, and Dionysus, the young dying gods of the Near East. All these symbolic attributes also occur in the Song of Songs, as characteristics of the *sponsus* as well as the *sponsa*. The vine, the grape, the vine flower, and the vineyard play a significant role here. The Beloved is like an apple-tree; she shall come down from the mountains (the cult places of the mother-goddess), "from the lions' dens, from the mountains of the leopards";[4] her womb is "an orchard of pomegranates, with pleasant fruits, camphire with spikenard, spikenard and saffron, calamus and cinnamon, with all trees of frankincense, myrrh and aloes, with all the chief spices."[5] Her hands "dropped

2 Ecclesïasticus 24 : 3–18 (AV mod.).
3 II Samuel 5 : 23f.   4 Song of Solomon 4 : 8 (AV).   5 4 : 13–15.

with myrrh" [6] (Adonis, we may remember, was born of the myrrh). Like the Holy Ghost, Wisdom is given as a gift to the elect, an idea that is taken up again in the doctrine of the Paraclete.

613   The pneumatic nature of Sophia as well as her world-building Maya character come out still more clearly in the apocryphal Wisdom of Solomon. "For wisdom is a loving spirit," [7] "kind to man." [8] She is "the worker of all things," "in her is an understanding spirit, holy." [9] She is "the breath of the power of God," "a pure effluence flowing from the glory of the Almighty," [10] "the brightness of the everlasting light, the unspotted mirror of the power of God," [11] a being "most subtil," who "passeth and goeth through all things by reason of her pureness." [12] She is "conversant with God," and "the Lord of all things himself loved her." [13] "Who of all that are is a more cunning workman than she?" [14] She is sent from heaven and from the throne of glory as a "Holy Spirit." [15] As a psychopomp she leads the way to God and assures immortality.[16]

614   The Wisdom of Solomon is emphatic about God's justice and, probably not without pragmatic purpose, ventures to sail very close to the wind: "Righteousness is immortal, but ungodly men with their works and words call death upon themselves." [17] The unrighteous and the ungodly, however, say:

> Let us oppress the poor righteous man,
>   let us not spare the widow,
>   nor reverence the ancient gray hairs of the aged.
> Let our strength be the law of justice:
>   for that which is feeble is found to be nothing worth.
> Therefore let us lie in wait for the righteous;
>   because . . . he upbraideth us with our offending the law,
>   and objecteth to our infamy. . . .
> He professeth to have the knowledge of God:
>   and he calleth himself the child of the Lord.
> He was made to reprove our thoughts.

· · · · · · · · · · · · · · · ·

---

[6] Song of Solomon 5 : 5.

[7] Wisdom of Solomon 1 : 6. (φιλάνθρωπον πνεῦμα σοφία.)   [8] 7 : 23.

[9] 7 : 22. (πάντων τεχνίτις./πνεῦμα νοερὸν ἅγιον.)   [10] 7 : 25 (AV mod.). (ἀπόρροια.)

[11] 7 : 26.   [12] 7 : 23, 24.   [13] 8 : 3. (συμβίωσιν ἔχουσα./πάντων δεσπότης.)

[14] 8 : 6.   [15] 9 : 10, 17.   [16] 6 : 18 and 8 : 13.   [17] 1 : 15–16 (mod.).

> Let us see if his words be true:
> and let us prove what shall happen in the end of him.
>
> .   .   .   .
>
> Let us examine him with despitefulness and torture,
> that we may know his meekness, and prove his patience.[18]

615   Where did we read but a short while before: "And the Lord said to Satan, Have you considered my servant Job, that there is none like him on the earth, a blameless and upright man, who fears God and turns away from evil? He still holds fast his integrity, although you moved me against him, to destroy him without cause"? "Wisdom is better than might," saith the Preacher.[19]

616   Not from mere thoughtfulness and unconsciousness, but from a deeper motive, the Wisdom of Solomon here touches on the sore spot. In order to understand this more fully, we would have to find out in what sort of relation the Book of Job stands to the change that occurred in the status of Yahweh at about the same time, i.e., its relation to the appearance of Sophia. It is not a question of literary history, but of Yahweh's fate as it affects man. From the ancient records we know that the divine drama was enacted between God and his people, who were betrothed to him, the masculine dynamis, like a woman, and over whose faithfulness he watched jealously. A particular instance of this is Job, whose faithfulness is subjected to a savage test. As I have said, the really astonishing thing is how easily Yahweh gives in to the insinuations of Satan. If it were true that he trusted Job perfectly, it would be only logical for Yahweh to defend him, unmask the malicious slanderer, and make him pay for his defamation of God's faithful servant. But Yahweh never thinks of it, not even after Job's innocence has been proved. We hear nothing of a rebuke or disapproval of Satan. Therefore, one cannot doubt Yahweh's connivance. His readiness to deliver Job into Satan's murderous hands proves that he doubts Job precisely because he projects his own tendency to unfaithfulness upon a scapegoat. There is reason to suspect that he is about to loosen his matrimonial ties with Israel but hides this intention from himself. This vaguely suspected unfaithfulness causes him, with the help of Satan, to seek out the unfaithful one, and he

18 2 : 10–19.   19 Job 2 : 3; Ecclesiastes 9 : 16.

[handwritten: LOT, OF SODOM + GOMORRAH]

infallibly picks on the most faithful of the lot, who is forthwith subjected to a gruelling test. Yahweh has become unsure of his own faithfulness.

617   At about the same time, or a little later, it is rumoured what has happened: he has remembered a feminine being who is no less agreeable to him than to man, a friend and playmate from the beginning of the world, the first-born of all God's creatures, a stainless reflection of his glory and a master workman, nearer and dearer to his heart than the late descendants of the proto- plast, the original man, who was but a secondary product stamped in his image. There must be some dire necessity re- sponsible for this anamnesis of Sophia: things simply could not go on as before, the "just" God could not go on committing in- justices, and the "Omniscient" could not behave any longer like a clueless and thoughtless human being. Self-reflection becomes an imperative necessity, and for this Wisdom is needed. Yahweh has to remember his absolute knowledge; for, if Job gains knowl- edge of God, then God must also learn to know himself. It just could not be that Yahweh's dual nature should become public property and remain hidden from himself alone. Whoever knows God has an effect on him. The failure of the attempt to corrupt Job has changed Yahweh's nature.

618   We shall now proceed to reconstruct, from the hints given in the Bible and from history, what happened after this change. For this purpose we must turn back to the time of Genesis, and to the protoplast before the Fall. He, Adam, produced Eve, his feminine counterpart, from his rib with the Creator's help, in the same way as the Creator had produced the hermaphroditic Adam from the *prima materia* and, along with him, the divinely stamped portion of humanity, namely the people of Israel and the other descendants of Adam.[20] Mysteriously following the same pattern, it was bound to happen that Adam's first son, like Satan, was an evildoer and murderer before the Lord, so that the prologue in heaven was repeated on earth. It can easily be sur- mised that this was the deeper reason why Yahweh gave special protection to the unsuccessful Cain, for he was a faithful repro- duction of Satan in miniature. Nothing is said about a proto- type of the early-departed Abel, who was dearer to God than

---

[20] [As to that portion of humanity *not* divinely stamped, and presumably de- scended from the pre-Adamic anthropoids, see par. 576, above.—EDITORS.]

Cain, the go-ahead husbandman (who was no doubt instructed in these arts by one of Satan's angels). Perhaps this prototype was another son of God of a more conservative nature than Satan, no rolling stone with a fondness for new and black-hearted thoughts, but one who was bound to the Father in child-like love, who harboured no other thoughts except those that enjoyed paternal approval, and who dwelt in the inner circle of the heavenly economy. That would explain why his earthly counterpart Abel could so soon "hasten away from the evil world," in the words of the Book of Wisdom, and return to the Father, while Cain in his earthly existence had to taste to the full the curse of his progressiveness on the one hand and of his moral inferiority on the other.

619   If the original father Adam is a copy of the Creator, his son Cain is certainly a copy of God's son Satan, and this gives us good reason for supposing that God's favourite, Abel, must also have his correspondence in a "supracelestial place." The ominous happenings that occur right at the beginning of a seemingly successful and satisfactory Creation—the Fall and the fratricide—catch our attention, and one is forced to admit that the initial situation, when the spirit of God brooded over the tohu-bohu, hardly permits us to expect an absolutely perfect result. Furthermore the Creator, who found every other day of his work "good," failed to give good marks to what happened on Monday. He simply said nothing—a circumstance that favours an argument from silence! What happened on that day was the final separation of the upper from the lower waters by the interposed "plate" of the firmament. It is clear that this unavoidable dualism refused, then as later, to fit smoothly into the concept of monotheism, because it points to a metaphysical disunity. This split, as we know from history, had to be patched up again and again through the centuries, concealed and denied. It had made itself felt from the very beginning in Paradise, through a strange inconsequence which befell the Creator or was put over on him. Instead of following his original programme of letting man appear on the last day as the most intelligent being and lord of all creatures, he created the serpent who proved to be much more intelligent and more conscious than Adam, and, in addition, had been created before him. We can hardly suppose that Yahweh would have played such a trick on himself; it is far more

likely that his son Satan had a hand in it. He is a trickster and
spoilsport who loves nothing better than to cause annoying acci-
dents. Although Yahweh had created the reptiles before Adam,
they were common or garden snakes, highly unintelligent, from
among whom Satan selected a tree-snake to use as his disguise.
From then on the rumour spread that the snake was "the most
spiritual animal." [21] Later the snake became the favourite symbol of the Nous, received high honours and was even permitted
to symbolize God's second son, because the latter was interpreted
as the world-redeeming Logos, which frequently appears as identical with the Nous. A legend of later origin maintains that the
snake in the Garden of Eden was Lilith, Adam's first wife, with
whom he begot a horde of demons. This legend likewise sup-
poses a trick that can hardly have been intended by the Creator.
Consequently, the Bible knows only of Eve as Adam's legitimate
wife. It nevertheless remains a strange fact that the original man
who was created in the image of God had, according to tradition, two wives, just like his heavenly prototype. Just as Yahweh
is legitimately united with his wife Israel, but has a feminine
pneuma as his intimate playmate from all eternity, so Adam first
has Lilith (the daughter or emanation of Satan) to wife, as a
Satanic correspondence to Sophia. Eve would then correspond
to the people of Israel. We naturally do not know why we should
hear at such a late date that the Ruach Elohim, the "spirit of
God," is not only feminine but a comparatively independent
being who exists side by side with God, and that long before the
marriage with Israel Yahweh had had relations with Sophia.
Nor do we know why, in the older tradition, the knowledge
of this first alliance had been lost. Likewise it was only quite
late that one heard of the delicate relationship between Adam
and Lilith. Whether Eve was as troublesome a wife for Adam
as the children of Israel, who were perpetually flirting with unfaithfulness, were for Yahweh, is equally dark to us. At any rate
the family life of our first parents was not all beer and skittles:
their first two sons are a typical pair of hostile brothers, for at
that time it was apparently still the custom to live out mythological motifs in reality. (Nowadays this is felt to be objectionable
and is denied whenever it happens.) The parents can share the
blame for original sin: Adam has only to remember his demon-

[21] τὸ πνευματικώτατον ζῷον.—A view that is found in Philo Judaeus.

princess, and Eve should never forget that she was the first to fall for the wiles of the serpent. Like the Fall, the Cain-Abel intermezzo can hardly be listed as one of Creation's shining successes. One must draw this conclusion because Yahweh himself did not appear to be informed in advance of the above-mentioned incidents. Here as later there is reason to suspect that no conclusions were ever drawn from Omniscience: Yahweh did not consult his total knowledge and was accordingly surprised by the result. One can observe the same phenomenon in human beings, wherever in fact people cannot deny themselves the pleasure of their emotions. It must be admitted that a fit of rage or a sulk has its secret attractions. Were that not so, most people would long since have acquired a little wisdom.

620   From this point of view we may be in a better position to understand what happened to Job. In the pleromatic or (as the Tibetans call it) Bardo state,[22] there is a perfect interplay of cosmic forces, but with the Creation—that is, with the division of the world into distinct processes in space and time—events begin to rub and jostle one another. Covered by the hem of the paternal mantle, Satan soon starts putting a right touch here and a wrong touch there, thus giving rise to complications which were apparently not intended in the Creator's plan and which come as surprises. While unconscious creation—animals, plants, and crystals—functions satisfactorily so far as we know, things are constantly going wrong with man. At first his consciousness is only a very little higher than that of the animals, for which reason his freedom of will is also extremely limited. But Satan takes an interest in him and experiments with him in his own way, leading him into all sorts of wickedness while his angels teach him the arts and sciences, which until now had been reserved for the perfection of the pleroma. (Even in those days Satan would have merited the name of "Lucifer"!) The peculiar, unforeseen antics of men arouse Yahweh's wrath and thereby involve him in his own creation. Divine interventions become a compelling necessity. Irritatingly enough, they only meet with temporary success. Even the Draconian punishment of drowning all life with a few choice exceptions (a fate which, according to old Johann Jacob Scheuchzer on the evidence of

22 [Cf. Jung's commentary on the *Tibetan Book of the Dead*, pars. 831ff.— EDITORS.]

the fossils, not even the fishes escaped), had no lasting effect. Creation remained just as tainted as before. The strange thing is that Yahweh invariably seeks the reason for this in man, who apparently refuses to obey, but never in his son, the father of all tricksters. This false orientation cannot fail to exasperate his already touchy nature, so that fear of God is regarded by man in general as the principle and even as the beginning of all wisdom. While mankind tried, under this hard discipline, to broaden their consciousness by acquiring a modicum of wisdom, that is, a little foresight and reflection,[23] it is clear from the historical development that Yahweh had lost sight of his pleromatic coexistence with Sophia since the days of the Creation. Her place was taken by the covenant with the chosen people, who were thus forced into the feminine role. At that time the people consisted of a patriarchal society in which women were only of secondary importance. God's marriage with Israel was therefore an essentially masculine affair, something like the founding of the Greek *polis,* which occurred about the same time. The inferiority of women was a settled fact. Woman was regarded as less perfect than man, as Eve's weakness for the blandishments of the serpent amply proved. *Perfection* is a masculine desideratum, while woman inclines by nature to *completeness.* And it is a fact that, even today, a man can stand a relative state of perfection much better and for a longer period than a woman, while as a rule it does not agree with women and may even be dangerous for them. If a woman strives for perfection she forgets the complementary role of completeness, which, though imperfect by itself, forms the necessary counterpart to perfection. For, just as completeness is always imperfect, so perfection is always incomplete, and therefore represents a final state which is hopelessly sterile. "Ex perfecto nihil fit," say the old masters, whereas the *imperfectum* carries within it the seeds of its own improvement. Perfectionism always ends in a blind alley, while completeness by itself lacks selective values.

621   At the bottom of Yahweh's marriage with Israel is a perfectionist intention which excludes that kind of relatedness we know as "Eros." The lack of Eros, of relationship to values, is painfully apparent in the Book of Job: the paragon of all creation is not a man but a monster! Yahweh has no Eros, no

23 Cf. φρονίμως in the parable of the unjust steward (Luke 16:8).

relationship to man, but only to a purpose man must help him fulfil. But that does not prevent him from being jealous and mistrustful like any other husband, though even here he has his purpose in mind and not man.

622   The faithfulness of his people becomes the more important to him the more he forgets Wisdom. But again and again they slip back into unfaithfulness despite the many proofs of his favour. This behaviour naturally does nothing to mollify Yahweh's jealousy and suspicions, hence Satan's insinuations fall on fertile ground when he drips his doubt about Job's faithfulness into the paternal ear. Against his own convictions Yahweh agrees without any hesitation to inflict the worst tortures on him. One misses Sophia's "love of mankind" more than ever. Even Job longs for the Wisdom which is nowhere to be found.[24]

623   Job marks the climax of this unhappy development. He epitomizes a thought which had been maturing in mankind about that time—a dangerous thought that makes great demands on the wisdom of gods and men. Though conscious of these demands, Job obviously does not know enough about the Sophia who is coeternal with God. Because man feels himself at the mercy of Yahweh's capricious will, he is in need of wisdom; not so Yahweh, who up to now has had nothing to contend with except man's nothingness. With the Job drama, however, the situation undergoes a radical change. Here Yahweh comes up against a man who stands firm, who clings to his rights until he is compelled to give way to brute force. He has seen God's face and the unconscious split in his nature. God was now known, and this knowledge went on working not only in Yahweh but in man too. Thus it was the men of the last few centuries before Christ who, at the gentle touch of the pre-existent Sophia, compensate Yahweh and his attitude, and at the same time complete the anamnesis of Wisdom. Taking a highly personified form that is clear proof of her autonomy, Wisdom reveals herself to men as a friendly helper and advocate against Yahweh, and shows them the bright side, the kind, just, and amiable aspect of their God.

624   At the time when Satan's practical joke with the snake compromised the paradise that was planned to be perfect, Yahweh

24 Job 28:12: "But where shall wisdom be found?" Whether this is a later interpolation or not makes no difference.

banished Adam and Eve, whom he had created as images of his masculine essence and its feminine emanation, to the extra-paradisal world, the limbo of "shards." It is not clear how much of Eve represents Sophia and how much of her is Lilith. At any rate Adam has priority in every respect. Eve was taken out of his body as an afterthought. I mention these details from Genesis only because the reappearance of Sophia in the heavenly regions points to a coming act of creation. She is indeed the "master workman"; she realizes God's thoughts by clothing them in material form, which is the prerogative of all feminine beings. Her coexistence with Yahweh signifies the perpetual *hieros gamos* from which worlds are begotten and born. A momentous change is imminent: God desires to regenerate himself in the mystery of the heavenly nuptials—as the chief gods of Egypt had done from time immemorial—and to become man. For this he uses the Egyptian model of the god's incarnation in Pharaoh, which in its turn is but a copy of the eternal *hieros gamos* in the pleroma. It would, however, be wrong to suppose that this archetype is merely repeating itself mechanically. So far as we know, this is never the case, since archetypal situations only return when specifically called for. The real reason for God's becoming man is to be sought in his encounter with Job. Later on we shall deal with this question in more detail.

IV

625   Just as the decision to become man apparently makes use of the ancient Egyptian model, so we can expect that the process itself will follow certain prefigurations. The approach of Sophia betokens a new creation. But this time it is not the world that is to be changed; rather it is God who intends to change his own nature. Mankind is not, as before, to be destroyed, but saved. In this decision we can discern the "philanthropic" influence of Sophia: no new human beings are to be created, but only one, the God-man. For this purpose a contrary procedure must be employed. The Second Adam shall not, like the first, proceed directly from the hand of the Creator, but shall be born of a human woman. So this time priority falls to the Second Eve, not only in a temporal sense but in a material sense as well. On the

basis of the so-called Proto-Evangelium, the Second Eve corresponds to "the woman and her seed" mentioned in Genesis 3 : 15, which shall bruise the serpent's head. And just as Adam was believed to be originally hermaphroditic, so "the woman and her seed" are thought of as a human pair, as the Queen of Heaven and Mother of God and as the divine son who has no human father. Thus Mary, the virgin, is chosen as the pure vessel for the coming birth of God. Her independence of the male is emphasized by her virginity as the *sine qua non* of the process. She is a "daughter of God" who, as a later dogma will establish, is distinguished at the outset by the privilege of an immaculate conception and is thus free from the taint of original sin. It is therefore evident that she belongs to the state before the Fall. This posits a new beginning. The divine immaculateness of her status makes it immediately clear that she not only bears the image of God in undiminished purity, but, as the bride of God, is also the incarnation of her prototype, namely Sophia. Her love of mankind, widely emphasized in the ancient writings, suggests that in this newest creation of his Yahweh has allowed himself to be extensively influenced by Sophia. For Mary, the blessed among women, is a friend and intercessor for sinners, which all men are. Like Sophia, she is a mediatrix who leads the way to God and assures man of immortality. Her Assumption is therefore the prototype of man's bodily resurrection. As the bride of God and Queen of Heaven she holds the place of the Old Testament Sophia.

626   Remarkable indeed are the unusual precautions which surround the making of Mary: immaculate conception, extirpation of the taint of sin, everlasting virginity. The Mother of God is obviously being protected against Satan's tricks. From this we can conclude that Yahweh has consulted his own omniscience, for in his omniscience there is a clear knowledge of the perverse intentions which lurk in the dark son of God. Mary must at all costs be protected from these corrupting influences. The inevitable consequence of all these elaborate protective measures is something that has not been sufficiently taken into account in the dogmatic evaluation of the Incarnation: her freedom from original sin sets Mary apart from mankind in general, whose common characteristic is original sin and therefore the need of redemption. The *status ante lapsum* is tantamount to a para-

disal, i.e., pleromatic and divine, existence. By having these special measures applied to her, Mary is elevated to the status of a goddess and consequently loses something of her humanity: she will not conceive her child in sin, like all other mothers, and therefore he also will never be a human being, but a god. To my knowledge at least, no one has ever perceived that this queers the pitch for a genuine Incarnation of God, or rather, that the Incarnation was only partially consummated. Both mother and son are not real human beings at all, but gods.

627 This arrangement, though it had the effect of exalting Mary's personality in the masculine sense by bringing it closer to the perfection of Christ, was at the same time injurious to the feminine principle of imperfection or completeness, since this was reduced by the perfectionizing tendency to the little bit of imperfection that still distinguishes Mary from Christ. *Phoebo propior lumina perdit!* Thus the more the feminine ideal is bent in the direction of the masculine, the more the woman loses her power to compensate the masculine striving for perfection, and a typically masculine, ideal state arises which, as we shall see, is threatened with an enantiodromia. No path leads beyond perfection into the future—there is only a turning back, a collapse of the ideal, which could easily have been avoided by paying attention to the feminine ideal of completeness. Yahweh's perfectionism is carried over from the Old Testament into the New, and despite all the recognition and glorification of the feminine principle this never prevailed against the patriarchal supremacy. We have not, therefore, by any means heard the last of it.

V

628 The older son of the first parents was corrupted by Satan and not much of a success. He was an eidolon of Satan, and only the younger son, Abel, was pleasing to God. In Cain the God-image was distorted, but in Abel it was considerably less dimmed. If Adam is thought of as a copy of God, then God's successful son, who served as a model for Abel (and about whom, as we have seen, there are no available documents), is the prefiguration of the God-man. Of the latter we know positively that, as

37

the Logos, he is preexistent and coeternal with God, indeed of the same substance (ὁμοούσιος) as he. One can therefore regard Abel as the imperfect prototype of God's son who is about to be begotten in Mary. Just as Yahweh originally undertook to create a chthonic equivalent of himself in the first man, Adam, so now he intends something similar, but much better. The extraordinary precautionary measures above-mentioned are designed to serve this purpose. The new son, Christ, shall on the one hand be a chthonic man like Adam, mortal and capable of suffering, but on the other hand he shall not be, like Adam, a mere copy, but God himself, begotten by himself as the Father, and rejuvenating the Father as the Son. As God he has always been God, and as the son of Mary, who is plainly a copy of Sophia, he is the Logos (synonymous with Nous), who, like Sophia, is a master workman, as stated by the Gospel according to St. John.[1] This identity of mother and son is borne out over and over again in the myths.

629   Although the birth of Christ is an event that occurred but once in history, it has always existed in eternity. For the layman in these matters, the identity of a nontemporal, eternal event with a unique historical occurrence is something that is extremely difficult to conceive. He must, however, accustom himself to the idea that "time" is a relative concept and needs to be complemented by that of the "simultaneous" existence, in the Bardo or pleroma, of all historical processes. What exists in the pleroma as an eternal process appears in time as an aperiodic sequence, that is to say, it is repeated many times in an irregular pattern. To take but one example: Yahweh had one good son and one who was a failure. Cain and Abel, Jacob and Esau, correspond to this prototype, and so, in all ages and in all parts of the world, does the motif of the hostile brothers, which in innumerable modern variants still causes dissension in families and keeps the psychotherapist busy. Just as many examples, no less instructive, could be found for the two women prefigured in eternity. When these things occur as modern variants, therefore, they should not be regarded merely as personal episodes, moods, or chance idiosyncrasies in people, but as fragments of the pleromatic process itself, which, broken up into individual

[1] John 1:3: "All things were made through him, and without him was not anything made that was made."

38

events occurring in time, is an essential component or aspect of the divine drama.

630   When Yahweh created the world from his *prima materia*, the "Void," he could not help breathing his own mystery into the Creation which is himself in every part, as every reasonable theology has long been convinced. From this comes the belief that it is possible to know God from his Creation. When I say that he could not help doing this, I do not imply any limitation of his omnipotence; on the contrary, it is an acknowledgment that all possibilities are contained in him, and that there are in consequence no other possibilities than those which express him.

631   All the world is God's, and God is in all the world from the very beginning. Why, then, the *tour de force* of the Incarnation? one asks oneself, astonished. God is in everything already, and yet there must be something missing if a sort of second entrance into Creation has now to be staged with so much care and circumspection. Since Creation is universal, reaching to the remotest stellar galaxies, and since it has also made organic life infinitely variable and capable of endless differentiation, we can hardly see where the defect lies. The fact that Satan has everywhere intruded his corrupting influence is no doubt regrettable for many reasons, but it makes no difference in principle. It is not easy to give an answer to this question. One would like to say that Christ had to appear in order to deliver mankind from evil. But when one considers that evil was originally slipped into the scheme of things by Satan, and still is, then it would seem much simpler if Yahweh would, for once, call this "practical joker" severely to account, get rid of his pernicious influence, and thus eliminate the root of all evil. He would then not need the elaborate arrangement of a special Incarnation with all the unforeseeable consequences which this entails. One should make clear to oneself what it means when God becomes man. It means nothing less than a world-shaking transformation of God. It means more or less what Creation meant in the beginning, namely an objectivation of God. At the time of the Creation he revealed himself in Nature; now he wants to be more specific and become man. It must be admitted, however, that there was a tendency in this direction right from the start. For, when those other human beings, who had evidently been created

39

before Adam, appeared on the scene along with the higher mammals, Yahweh created on the following day, by a special act of creation, a man who was the image of God. This was the first prefiguration of his becoming man. He took Adam's descendants, especially the people of Israel, into his personal possession, and from time to time he filled this people's prophets with his spirit. All these things were preparatory events and symptoms of a tendency within God to become man. But in omniscience there had existed from all eternity a knowledge of the human nature of God or of the divine nature of man. That is why, long before Genesis was written, we find corresponding testimonies in the ancient Egyptian records. These intimations and prefigurations of the Incarnation must strike one as either completely incomprehensible or superfluous, since all creation *ex nihilo* is God's and consists of nothing but God, with the result that man, like the rest of creation, is simply God become concrete. Prefigurations, however, are not in themselves creative events, but are only stages in the process of becoming conscious. It was only quite late that we realized (or rather, are beginning to realize) that God is Reality itself and therefore—last but not least—man. This realization is a millennial process.

VI

632   In view of the immense problem which we are about to discuss, this excursus on pleromatic events is not out of place as an introduction.

633   What, then, is the real reason for the Incarnation as an historical event?

634   In order to answer this question we have to go rather far back. As we have seen, Yahweh evidently has a disinclination to take his absolute knowledge into account as a counterbalance to the dynamism of omnipotence. The most instructive example of this is his relation to Satan: it always looks as if Yahweh were completely uninformed about his son's intentions. That is because he never consults his omniscience. We can only explain this on the assumption that Yahweh was so fascinated by his successive acts of creation, so taken up with them, that he forgot about his omniscience altogether. It is quite understandable

that the magical bodying forth of the most diverse objects, which had never before existed in such pristine splendour, should have caused God infinite delight. Sophia's memory is not at fault when she says:

> when he marked out the foundations of the earth,
>   then I was by him, like a master workman,
> and I was daily his delight.[1]

635   The Book of Job still rings with the proud joy of creating when Yahweh points to the huge animals he has successfully turned out:

> Behold, Behemoth,
>   which I made as I made you.
>
>   .   .   .   .
>
> He is the first of the works of God,
>   made to be lord over his companions.[2]

636   So even in Job's day Yahweh is still intoxicated with the tremendous power and grandeur of his creation. Compared with this, what are Satan's pinpricks and the lamentations of human beings who were created with the behemoth, even if they do bear God's image? Yahweh seems to have forgotten this fact entirely, otherwise he would never have ridden so roughshod over Job's human dignity.

637   It is only the careful and farsighted preparations for Christ's birth which show us that omniscience has begun to have a noticeable effect on Yahweh's actions. A certain philanthropic and universalistic tendency makes itself felt. The "children of Israel" take something of a second place in comparison with the "children of men." After Job, we hear nothing further about new covenants. Proverbs and gnomic utterances seem to be the order of the day, and a real *novum* now appears on the scene, namely apocalyptic communications. This points to metaphysical acts of cognition, that is, to "constellated" unconscious contents which are ready to irrupt into consciousness. In all this, as we have said, we discern the helpful hand of Sophia.

638   If we consider Yahweh's behaviour, up to the reappearance of Sophia, as a whole, one indubitable fact strikes us—the fact

---

[1] Proverbs 8 : 29–30.   [2] Job 40 : 15, 19 (last line, ZB).

that his actions are accompanied by an inferior consciousness. Time and again we miss reflection and regard for absolute knowledge. His consciousness seems to be not much more than a primitive "awareness" which knows no reflection and no morality. One merely perceives and acts blindly, without conscious inclusion of the subject, whose individual existence raises no problems. Today we would call such a state psychologically "unconscious," and in the eyes of the law it would be described as *non compos mentis*. The fact that consciousness does not perform acts of thinking does not, however, prove that they do not exist. They merely occur unconsciously and make themselves felt indirectly in dreams, visions, revelations, and "instinctive" changes of consciousness, whose very nature tells us that they derive from an "unconscious" knowledge and are the result of unconscious acts of judgment or unconscious conclusions.

639   Some such process can be observed in the curious change which comes over Yahweh's behaviour after the Job episode. There can be no doubt that he did not immediately become conscious of the moral defeat he had suffered at Job's hands. In his omniscience, of course, this fact had been known from all eternity, and it is not unthinkable that the knowledge of it unconsciously brought him into the position of dealing so harshly with Job in order that he himself should become conscious of something through this conflict, and thus gain new insight. Satan who, with good reason, later on received the name of "Lucifer," knew how to make more frequent and better use of omniscience than did his father.[3] It seems he was the only one among the sons of God who developed that much initiative. At all events, it was he who placed those unforeseen incidents in Yahweh's way, which omniscience knew to be necessary and indeed indispensable for the unfolding and completion of the divine drama. Among these the case of Job was decisive, and it could only have happened thanks to Satan's initiative.

640   The victory of the vanquished and oppressed is obvious:

---

[3] In Christian tradition, too, there is a belief that God's intention to become man was known to the Devil many centuries before, and that this was why he instilled the Dionysus myth into the Greeks, so that they could say, when the joyful tidings reached them in reality: "So what? We knew all that long ago." When the conquistadores later discovered the crosses of the Mayas in Yucatán, the Spanish bishops used the same argument.

Job stands morally higher than Yahweh. In this respect the creature has surpassed the creator. As always when an external event
touches on some unconscious knowledge, this knowledge can
reach consciousness. The event is recognized as a *déjà vu,* and
one remembers a pre-existent knowledge about it. Something
of the kind must have happened to Yahweh. Job's superiority
cannot be shrugged off. Hence a situation arises in which real
reflection is needed. That is why Sophia steps in. She reinforces
the much needed self-reflection and thus makes possible Yahweh's decision to become man. It is a decision fraught with consequences: he raises himself above his earlier primitive level of
consciousness by indirectly acknowledging that the man Job is
morally superior to him and that therefore he has to catch up
and become human himself. Had he not taken this decision he
would have found himself in flagrant opposition to his omniscience. Yahweh must become man precisely because he has done
man a wrong. He, the guardian of justice, knows that every
wrong must be expiated, and Wisdom knows that moral law is
above even him. Because his creature has surpassed him he
must regenerate himself.

641   As nothing can happen without a pre-existing pattern, not
even creation *ex nihilo,* which must always resort to the treasure-
house of eternal images in the fabulous mind of the "master
workman," the choice of a model for the son who is now about
to be begotten lies between Adam (to a limited extent) and Abel
(to a much greater extent). Adam's limitation lies in the fact
that, even if he is the Anthropos, he is chiefly a creature and a
father. Abel's advantage is that he is the son well pleasing to
God, begotten and not directly created. One disadvantage has
to be accepted: he met with an early death by violence, too
early to leave behind him a widow and children, which ought
really to be part of human fate if lived to the full. Abel is not the
authentic archetype of the son well pleasing to God; he is a
copy, but the first of the kind to be met with in the Scriptures.
The young dying god is also well known in the contemporary
pagan religions, and so is the fratricide motif. We shall hardly
be wrong in assuming that Abel's fate refers back to a metaphysical event which was played out between Satan and another
son of God with a "light" nature and more devotion to his
father. Egyptian tradition can give us information on this point

43

and Set). As we have said, the disadvantage prefigured
Abel type can hardly be avoided, because it is an integral
part of the mythical-son drama, as the numerous pagan variants
of this motif show. The short, dramatic course of Abel's fate
serves as an excellent paradigm for the life and death of a God
become man.

642   To sum up: the immediate cause of the Incarnation lies in
Job's elevation, and its purpose is the differentiation of Yahweh's consciousness. For this a situation of extreme gravity was
needed, a *peripeteia* charged with affect, without which no
higher level of consciousness can be reached.

VII

643   In addition to Abel, we have to consider, as a model for the
impending birth of the son of God, the general pattern of the
hero's life which has been established since time immemorial
and handed down by tradition. Since this son is not intended
merely as a national Messiah, but as the universal saviour of
mankind, we have also to consider the pagan myths and revelations concerning the life of one who is singled out by the gods.

644   The birth of Christ is therefore characterized by all the usual
phenomena attendant upon the birth of a hero, such as the annunciation, the divine generation from a virgin, the coinci-
dence of the birth with the thrice-repeated *coniunctio maxima*
(♃ ♂ ♄) in the sign of Pisces, which at that precise moment
inaugurated the new era, the recognition of the birth of a king,
the persecution of the newborn, his flight and concealment, his
lowly birth, etc. The motif of the growing up of the hero is dis-
cernible in the wisdom of the twelve-year-old child in the
temple, and there are several examples in the gospels of the
breaking away from the mother.

645   It goes without saying that a quite special interest attaches
to the character and fate of the incarnate son of God. Seen from
a distance of nearly two thousand years, it is uncommonly difficult to reconstruct a biographical picture of Christ from the
traditions that have been preserved. Not a single text is extant
which would fulfil even the minimum modern requirements
for writing a history. The historically verifiable facts are ex-

tremely scanty, and the little biographically valid material that exists is not sufficient for us to create out of it a consistent career or an even remotely probable character. Certain theologians have discovered the main reason for this in the fact that Christ's biography and psychology cannot be separated from eschatology. Eschatology means in effect that Christ is God and man at the same time and that he therefore suffers a divine as well as a human fate. The two natures interpenetrate so thoroughly that any attempt to separate them mutilates both. The divine overshadows the human, and the human being is scarcely graspable as an empirical personality. Even the critical procedures of modern psychology do not suffice to throw light on all the obscurities. Every attempt to single out one particular feature for clarity's sake does violence to another which is just as essential either with respect to his divinity or with respect to his humanity. The commonplace is so interwoven with the miraculous and the mythical that we can never be sure of our facts. Perhaps the most disturbing and confusing thing of all is that the oldest writings, those of St. Paul, do not seem to have the slightest interest in Christ's existence as a concrete human being. The synoptic gospels are equally unsatisfactory as they have more the character of propaganda than of biography.

646   With regard to the human side of Christ, if we can speak of a "purely human" aspect at all, what stands out particularly clearly is his love of mankind. This feature is already implied in the relationship of Mary to Sophia, and especially in his genesis by the Holy Ghost, whose feminine nature is personified by Sophia, since she is the preliminary historical form of the ἅγιον πνεῦμα, who is symbolized by the dove, the bird belonging to the love-goddess. Furthermore, the love-goddess is in most cases the mother of the young dying god. Christ's love of mankind is, however, limited to a not inconsiderable degree by a certain predestinarian tendency which sometimes causes him to withhold his salutary message from those who do not belong to the elect. If one takes the doctrine of predestination literally, it is difficult to see how it can be fitted into the framework of the Christian message. But taken psychologically, as a means to achieving a definite effect, it can readily be understood that these allusions to predestination give one a feeling of distinction. If one knows that one has been singled out by divine choice

45

tention from the beginning of the world, then one feels
)eyond the transitoriness and meaninglessness of ordinary
existence and transported to a new state of dignity and
importance, like one who has a part in the divine world drama.
In this way man is brought nearer to God, and this is in entire
accord with the meaning of the message in the gospels.

647   Besides his love of mankind a certain irascibility is noticeable in Christ's character, and, as is often the case with people
of emotional temperament, a manifest lack of self-reflection.
There is no evidence that Christ ever wondered about himself,
or that he ever confronted himself. To this rule there is only
one significant exception—the despairing cry from the Cross:
"My God, my God, why hast thou forsaken me?" Here his
human nature attains divinity; at that moment God experiences
what it means to be a mortal man and drinks to the dregs what
he made his faithful servant Job suffer. Here is given the answer
to Job, and, clearly, this supreme moment is as divine as it is
human, as "eschatological" as it is "psychological." And at this
moment, too, where one can feel the human being so absolutely,
the divine myth is present in full force. And both mean one
and the same thing. How, then, can one possibly "demytholo-
gize" the figure of Christ? A rationalistic attempt of that sort
would soak all the mystery out of his personality, and what remained would no longer be the birth and tragic fate of a God
in time, but, historically speaking, a badly authenticated religious teacher, a Jewish reformer who was hellenistically interpreted and misunderstood—a kind of Pythagoras, maybe, or, if
you like, a Buddha or a Mohammed, but certainly not a son of
God or a God incarnate. Nor does anybody seem to have realized
what would be the consequences of a Christ disinfected of all
trace of eschatology. Today we have an empirical psychology,
which continues to exist despite the fact that the theologians
have done their best to ignore it, and with its help we can put
certain of Christ's statements under the microscope. If these
statements are detached from their mythical context, they can
only be explained personalistically. But what sort of conclusion
are we bound to arrive at if a statement like "I am the way, and
the truth, and the life; no one comes to the Father, but by me" [1]
is reduced to personal psychology? Obviously the same con-

1 John 14:6.

clusion as that reached by Jesus' relatives when, in their ignorance of eschatology, they said, "He is beside himself." [2] What
is the use of a religion without a mythos, since religion means,
if anything at all, precisely that function which links us back to
the eternal myth?

648   In view of these portentous impossibilities, it has been assumed, perhaps as the result of a growing impatience with the
difficult factual material, that Christ was nothing but a myth, in
this case no more than a fiction. But myth is not fiction: it consists of facts that are continually repeated and can be observed
over and over again. It is something that happens to man, and
men have mythical fates just as much as the Greek heroes do.
The fact that the life of Christ is largely myth does absolutely
nothing to disprove its factual truth—quite the contrary. I would
even go so far as to say that the mythical character of a life is just
what expresses its universal human validity. It is perfectly possible, psychologically, for the unconscious or an archetype to
take complete possession of a man and to determine his fate
down to the smallest detail. At the same time objective, non-
psychic parallel phenomena can occur which also represent the
archetype. It not only seems so, it simply is so, that the archetype
fulfils itself not only psychically in the individual, but objectively outside the individual. My own conjecture is that Christ
was such a personality. The life of Christ is just what it had to
be if it is the life of a god and a man at the same time. It is a
symbolum, a bringing together of heterogeneous natures, rather
as if Job and Yahweh were combined in a single personality.
Yahweh's intention to become man, which resulted from his
collision with Job, is fulfilled in Christ's life and suffering.

VIII

649   When one remembers the earlier acts of creation, one won-
ders what has happened to Satan and his subversive activities.
Everywhere he sows his tares among the wheat. One suspects he
had a hand in Herod's massacre of the innocents. What is certain is his attempt to lure Christ into the role of a worldly ruler.
Equally obvious is the fact, as is evidenced by the remarks of

[2] Mark 3:21.

47

the man possessed of devils, that he is very well informed about Christ's nature. He also seems to have inspired Judas, without, however, being able to influence or prevent the sacrificial death.

650   His comparative ineffectiveness can be explained on the one hand by the careful preparations for the divine birth, and on the other hand by a curious metaphysical phenomenon which Christ witnessed: he saw Satan fall like lightning from heaven.[1] In this vision a metaphysical event has become temporal; it indicates the historic and—so far as we know—final separation of Yahweh from his dark son. Satan is banished from heaven and no longer has any opportunity to inveigle his father into dubious undertakings. This event may well explain why he plays such an inferior role wherever he appears in the history of the Incarnation. His role here is in no way comparable to his former confidential relationship to Yahweh. He has obviously forfeited the paternal affection and been exiled. The punishment which we missed in the story of Job has at last caught up with him, though in a strangely limited form. Although he is banished from the heavenly court he has kept his dominion over the sublunary world. He is not cast directly into hell, but upon earth. Only at the end of time shall he be locked up and made permanently ineffective. Christ's death cannot be laid at his door, because, through its prefiguration in Abel and in the young dying gods, the sacrificial death was a fate chosen by Yahweh as a reparation for the wrong done to Job on the one hand, and on the other hand as a fillip to the spiritual and moral development of man. There can be no doubt that man's importance is enormously enhanced if God himself deigns to become one.

651   As a result of the partial neutralization of Satan, Yahweh identifies with his light aspect and becomes the good God and loving father. He has not lost his wrath and can still mete out punishment, but he does it with justice. Cases like the Job tragedy are apparently no longer to be expected. He proves himself benevolent and gracious. He shows mercy to the sinful children of men and is defined as Love itself. But although Christ has complete confidence in his father and even feels at one with him, he cannot help inserting the cautious petition—and warning—into the Lord's Prayer: "Lead us not into tempta-

[1] Luke 10:18.

tion, but deliver us from evil." God is asked not to entice us outright into doing evil, but rather to deliver us from it. The possibility that Yahweh, in spite of all the precautionary measures and in spite of his express intention to become the Summum Bonum, might yet revert to his former ways is not so remote that one need not keep one eye open for it. At any rate, Christ considers it appropriate to remind his father of his destructive inclinations towards mankind and to beg him to desist from them. Judged by any human standards it is after all unfair, indeed extremely immoral, to entice little children into doing things that might be dangerous for them, simply in order to test their moral stamina! Especially as the difference between a child and a grown-up is immeasurably smaller than that between God and his creatures, whose moral weakness is particularly well known to him. The incongruity of it is so colossal that if this petition were not in the Lord's Prayer one would have to call it sheer blasphemy, because it really will not do to ascribe such contradictory behaviour to the God of Love and Summum Bonum.

652   The sixth petition indeed allows a deep insight, for in face of this fact Christ's immense certainty with regard to his father's character becomes somewhat questionable. It is, unfortunately, a common experience that particularly positive and categorical assertions are met with wherever there is a slight doubt in the background that has to be stifled. One must admit that it would be contrary to all reasonable expectations to suppose that a God who, for all his lavish generosity, had been subject to intermittent but devastating fits of rage ever since time began could suddenly become the epitome of everything good. Christ's unadmitted but none the less evident doubt in this respect is confirmed in the New Testament, and particularly in the Apocalypse. There Yahweh again delivers himself up to an unheard-of fury of destruction against the human race, of whom a mere hundred and forty-four thousand specimens appear to survive.[2]

653   One is indeed at a loss how to bring such a reaction into line with the behaviour of a loving father, whom we would expect to glorify his creation with patience and love. It looks as if the attempt to secure an absolute and final victory for good is bound to lead to a dangerous accumulation of evil and hence to catas-

[2] Revelation 7:4.

49

trophe. Compared with the end of the world, the destruction of Sodom and Gomorrah and even the Deluge are mere child's play; for this time the whole of creation goes to pieces. As Satan was locked up for a time, then conquered and cast into a lake of fire,[3] the destruction of the world can hardly be the work of the devil, but must be an "act of God" not influenced by Satan.

654   The end of the world is, however, preceded by the circumstance that even Christ's victory over his brother Satan—Abel's counterstroke against Cain—is not really and truly won, because, before this can come to pass, a final and mighty manifestation of Satan is to be expected. One can hardly suppose that God's incarnation in his son Christ would be calmly accepted by Satan. It must certainly have stirred up his jealousy to the highest pitch and evoked in him a desire to imitate Christ (a role for which he is particularly well suited as the πνεῦμα ἀντίμιμον), and to become incarnate in his turn as the *dark* God. (As we know, numerous legends were later woven round this theme.) This plan will be put into operation by the figure of the Antichrist after the preordained thousand years are over, the term allotted by astrology to the reign of Christ. This expectation, which is already to be found in the New Testament, reveals a doubt as to the immediate finality or universal effectiveness of the work of salvation. Unfortunately it must be said that these expectations gave rise to thoughtless revelations which were never even discussed with other aspects of the doctrine of salvation, let alone brought into harmony with them.

IX

655   I mention these future apocalyptic events only to illustrate the doubt which is indirectly expressed in the sixth petition of the Lord's Prayer, and not in order to give a general interpretation of the Apocalypse. I shall come back to this theme later on. But, before doing so, we must turn to the question of how matters stood with the Incarnation after the death of Christ. We have always been taught that the Incarnation was a unique historical event. No repetition of it was to be expected, any more than one could expect a further revelation of the Logos, for this

3 Revelation 19:20.

too was included in the uniqueness of God's appearance on earth, in human form, nearly two thousand years ago. The sole source of revelation, and hence the final authority, is the Bible. God is an authority only in so far as he authorized the writings in the New Testament, and with the conclusion of the New Testament the authentic communications of God cease. Thus far the Protestant standpoint. The Catholic Church, the direct heir and continuator of historical Christianity, proves to be somewhat more cautious in this regard, believing that with the assistance of the Holy Ghost the dogma can progressively develop and unfold. This view is in entire agreement with Christ's own teachings about the Holy Ghost and hence with the further continuance of the Incarnation. Christ is of the opinion that whoever believes in him—believes, that is to say, that he is the son of God—can "do the works that I do, and greater works than these." [1] He reminds his disciples that he had told them they were gods.[2] The believers or chosen ones are children of God and "fellow heirs with Christ." [3] When Christ leaves the earthly stage, he will ask his father to send his flock a Counsellor (the "Paraclete"), who will abide with them and in them for ever.[4] The Counsellor is the Holy Ghost, who will be sent from the father. This "Spirit of truth" will teach the believers "all things" and guide them "into all truth." [5] According to this, Christ envisages a continuing realization of God in his children, and consequently in his (Christ's) brothers and sisters in the spirit, so that his own works need not necessarily be considered the greatest ones.

656   Since the Holy Ghost is the Third Person of the Trinity and God is present entire in each of the three Persons at any time, the indwelling of the Holy Ghost means nothing less than an approximation of the believer to the status of God's son. One can therefore understand what is meant by the remark "you are gods." The deifying effect of the Holy Ghost is naturally assisted by the *imago Dei* stamped on the elect. God, in the shape of the Holy Ghost, puts up his tent in man, for he is obviously minded to realize himself continually not only in Adam's descendants, but in an indefinitely large number of believers, and possibly in mankind as a whole. Symptomatic of this is the

1 John 14:12.   2 10:34.   3 Romans 8:17.   4 John 14:16f.
5 14:26 and 16:13.

51

significant fact that Barnabas and Paul were identified in Lystra with Zeus and Hermes: "The gods have come down to us in the likeness of men." [6] This was certainly only the more naïve, pagan view of the Christian transmutation, but precisely for that reason it convinces. Tertullian must have had something of the sort in mind when he described the "sublimiorem Deum" as a sort of lender of divinity "who has made gods of men." [7]

657　God's Incarnation in Christ requires continuation and completion because Christ, owing to his virgin birth and his sinlessness, was not an empirical human being at all. As stated in the first chapter of St. John, he represented a light which, though it shone in the darkness, was not comprehended by the darkness. He remained outside and above mankind. Job, on the other hand, was an ordinary human being, and therefore the wrong done to him, and through him to mankind, can, according to divine justice, only be repaired by an incarnation of God in an empirical human being. This act of expiation is performed by the Paraclete; for, just as man must suffer from God, so God must suffer from man. Otherwise there can be no reconciliation between the two.

658　The continuing, direct operation of the Holy Ghost on those who are called to be God's children implies, in fact, a broadening process of incarnation. Christ, the son begotten by God, is the first-born who is succeeded by an ever-increasing number of younger brothers and sisters. These are, however, neither begotten by the Holy Ghost nor born of a virgin. This may be prejudicial to their metaphysical status, but their merely human birth will in no sense endanger their prospects of a future position of honour at the heavenly court, nor will it diminish their capacity to perform miracles. Their lowly origin (possibly from the mammals) does not prevent them from entering into a close kinship with God as their father and Christ as their brother. In a metaphorical sense, indeed, it is actually a "kinship by blood," since they have received their share of the blood and flesh of Christ, which means more than mere adoption. These profound changes in man's status are the direct result of Christ's work of redemption. Redemption or deliverance has several different aspects,

[6] Acts 14:11.

[7] "Mancipem quendam divinitatis qui ex hominibus deos fecerit." *Apologeticus,* XI, in Migne, *P.L.,* vol. 1, col. 386.

the most important of which is the expiation wrought by Christ's sacrificial death for the misdemeanours of mankind. His blood cleanses us from the evil consequences of sin. He reconciles God with man and delivers him from the divine wrath, which hangs over him like doom, and from eternal damnation. It is obvious that such ideas still picture God the father as the dangerous Yahweh who has to be propitiated. The agonizing death of his son is supposed to give him satisfaction for an affront he has suffered, and for this "moral injury" he would be inclined to take a terrible vengeance. Once more we are appalled by the incongruous attitude of the world creator towards his creatures, who to his chagrin never behave according to his expectations. It is as if someone started a bacterial culture which turned out to be a failure. He might curse his luck, but he would never seek the reason for the failure in the bacilli and want to punish them morally for it. Rather, he would select a more suitable culture medium. Yahweh's behaviour towards his creatures contradicts all the requirements of so-called "divine" reason whose possession is supposed to distinguish men from animals. Moreover, a bacteriologist might make a mistake in his choice of a culture medium, for he is only human. But God in his omniscience would never make mistakes if only he consulted with it. He has equipped his human creatures with a modicum of consciousness and a corresponding degree of free will, but he must also know that by so doing he leads them into the temptation of falling into a dangerous independence. That would not be too great a risk if man had to do with a creator who was only kind and good. But Yahweh is forgetting his son Satan, to whose wiles even he occasionally succumbs. How then could he expect man with his limited consciousness and imperfect knowledge to do any better? He also overlooks the fact that the more consciousness a man possesses the more he is separated from his instincts (which at least give him an inkling of the hidden wisdom of God) and the more prone he is to error. He is certainly not up to Satan's wiles if even his creator is unable, or unwilling, to restrain this powerful spirit.

X

659   The fact of God's "unconsciousness" throws a peculiar light
on the doctrine of salvation. Man is not so much delivered from
his sins, even if he is baptized in the prescribed manner and thus
washed clean, as delivered from fear of the consequences of sin,
that is, from the wrath of God. Consequently, the work of salvation is intended to save man from the fear of God. This is
certainly possible where the belief in a loving father, who has
sent his only-begotten son to rescue the human race, has re-
pressed the persistent traces of the old Yahweh and his dangerous
affects. Such a belief, however, presupposes a lack of reflection
or a *sacrificium intellectus,* and it appears questionable whether
either of them can be morally justified. We should never forget
that it was Christ himself who taught us to make usurious use of
the talents entrusted to us and not hide them in the ground. One
ought not to make oneself out to be more stupid and more unconscious than one really is, for in all other aspects we are called
upon to be alert, critical, and self-aware, so as not to fall into
temptation, and to "examine the spirits" who want to gain influence over us and "see whether they are of God," [1] so that we may
recognize the mistakes we make. It even needs superhuman in-
telligence to avoid the cunning snares of Satan. These obligations inevitably sharpen our understanding, our love of truth,
and the urge to know, which as well as being genuine human
virtues are quite possibly effects of that spirit which "searches
everything, even the depths of God." [2] These intellectual and
moral capacities are themselves of a divine nature, and therefore
cannot and must not be cut off. It is just by following Christian
morality that one gets into the worst collisions of duty. Only
those who habitually make five an even number can escape them.
The fact that Christian ethics leads to collisions of duty speaks in
its favour. By engendering insoluble conflicts and consequently
an *afflictio animae,* it brings man nearer to a knowledge of God.
All opposites are of God, therefore man must bend to this burden; and in so doing he finds that God in his "oppositeness" has
taken possession of him, incarnated himself in him. He becomes
a vessel filled with divine conflict. We rightly associate the idea

[1] I John 4: 1 (mod.).   [2] I Corinthians 2: 10.

54

of suffering with a state in which the opposites violently collide
with one another, and we hesitate to describe such a painful
experience as being "redeemed." Yet it cannot be denied that
the great symbol of the Christian faith, the Cross, upon which
hangs the suffering figure of the Redeemer, has been emphatically held up before the eyes of Christians for nearly two thousand years. This picture is completed by the two thieves, one of
whom goes down to hell, the other into paradise. One could
hardly imagine a better representation of the "oppositeness"
of the central Christian symbol. Why this inevitable product
of Christian psychology should signify redemption is difficult
to see, except that the conscious recognition of the opposites,
painful though it may be at the moment, does bring with it a
definite feeling of deliverance. It is on the one hand a deliverance from the distressing state of dull and helpless unconsciousness, and on the other hand a growing awareness of God's oppositeness, in which man can participate if he does not shrink from
being wounded by the dividing sword which is Christ. Only
through the most extreme and most menacing conflict does the
Christian experience deliverance into divinity, always provided
that he does not break, but accepts the burden of being marked
out by God. In this way alone can the *imago Dei* realize itself in
him, and God become man. The seventh petition in the Lord's
Prayer, "But deliver us from evil," is to be understood in the
same sense as Christ's prayer in the Garden of Gethsemane:
"My Father, if it be possible, let this cup pass from me." [3] In
principle it does not seem to fit God's purpose to exempt a man
from conflict and hence from evil. It is altogether human to express such a desire but it must not be made into a principle,
because it is directed against God's will and rests only on human
weakness and fear. Fear is certainly justified up to a point, for,
to make the conflict complete, there must be doubt and uncertainty as to whether man's strength is not being overtaxed.

660   Because the *imago Dei* pervades the whole human sphere
and makes mankind its involuntary exponent, it is just possible
that the four-hundred-year-old schism in the Church and the
present division of the political world into two hostile camps
are both expressions of the unrecognized polarity of the domi-
nant archetype.

3 Matthew 26:39.

661   The traditional view of Christ's work of redemption reflects a one-sided way of thinking, no matter whether we regard that one-sidedness as purely human or as willed by God. The other view, which regards the atonement not as the payment of a human debt to God, but as reparation for a wrong done by God to man, has been briefly outlined above. This view seems to me to be better suited to the power situation as it actually exists. The sheep can stir up mud in the wolf's drinking water, but can do him no other harm. So also the creature can disappoint the creator, but it is scarcely credible that he can do him a painful wrong. This lies only in the power of the creator with respect to the powerless creature. On this view, a wrong is imputed to God, but it is certainly no worse than what has already been imputed to him if one assumes that it was necessary to torture the son to death on the Cross merely in order to appease the father's wrath. What kind of father is it who would rather his son were slaughtered than forgive his ill-advised creatures who have been corrupted by his precious Satan? What is supposed to be demonstrated by this gruesome and archaic sacrifice of the son? God's love, perhaps? Or his implacability? We know from chapter 22 of Genesis [4] and from Exodus 22 : 29 that Yahweh has a tendency to employ such means as the killing of the son and the first-born in order to test his people's faith or to assert his will, despite the fact that his omniscience and omnipotence have no need whatever of such savage procedures, which moreover set a bad example to the mighty ones of the earth. It is very understandable, therefore, that a naïve mind is apt to run away from such questions and excuse this manoeuvre as a beautiful *sacrificium intellectus*. If one prefers not to read the Eighty-ninth Psalm, the matter will not end there. He who cheats once will cheat again, particularly when it comes to self-knowledge. But self-knowledge, in the form of an examination of conscience, is demanded by Christian ethics. They were very pious people who maintained that self-knowledge paves the way to knowledge of God.

4 Abraham and Isaac.

XI

662   To believe that God is the Summum Bonum is impossible for a reflecting consciousness. Such a consciousness does not feel in any way delivered from the fear of God, and therefore asks itself, quite rightly, what Christ means to it. That, indeed, is the great question: can Christ still be interpreted in our day and age, or must one be satisfied with the historical interpretation?

663   One thing, anyway, cannot be doubted: Christ is a highly numinous figure. The interpretation of him as God and the son of God is in full accord with this. The old view, which is based on Christ's own view of the matter, asserts that he came into the world, suffered, and died in order to save mankind from the wrath to come. Furthermore he believed that his own bodily resurrection would assure all God's children of the same future.

664   We have already pointed out at some length how curiously God's salvationist project works out in practice. All he does is, in the shape of his own son, to rescue mankind from himself. This thought is as scurrilous as the old rabbinical view of Yahweh hiding the righteous from his wrath under his throne, where of course he cannot see them. It is exactly as if God the father were a different God from the son, which is not the meaning at all. Nor is there any psychological need for such an assumption, since the undoubted lack of reflection in God's consciousness is sufficient to explain his peculiar behaviour. It is quite right, therefore, that fear of God should be considered the beginning of all wisdom. On the other hand, the much-vaunted goodness, love, and justice of God should not be regarded as mere propitiation, but should be recognized as a genuine experience, for God is a *coincidentia oppositorum*. Both are justified, the fear of God as well as the love of God.

665   A more differentiated consciousness must, sooner or later, find it difficult to love, as a kind father, a God whom on account of his unpredictable fits of wrath, his unreliability, injustice, and cruelty, it has every reason to fear. The decay of the gods of antiquity has proved to our satisfaction that man does not relish any all-too-human inconsistencies and weaknesses in his gods. Likewise, it is probable that Yahweh's moral defeat in his dealings with Job had its hidden effects: man's unintended

elevation on the one hand, and on the other hand a disturbance of the unconscious. For a while the first-mentioned effect remains a mere fact, not consciously realized though registered by the unconscious. This contributes to the disturbance in the unconscious, which thereby acquires a higher potential than exists in consciousness. Man then counts for more in the unconscious than he does consciously. In these circumstances the potential starts flowing from the unconscious towards consciousness, and the unconscious breaks through in the form of dreams, visions, and revelations. Unfortunately the Book of Job cannot be dated with any certainty. As mentioned above, it was written somewhere between 600 and 300 B.C. During the first half of the sixth century, Ezekiel,[1] the prophet with the so-called "pathological" features, appears on the scene. Although laymen are inclined to apply this epithet to his visions, I must, as a psychiatrist, emphatically state that visions and their accompanying phenomena cannot be uncritically evaluated as morbid. Visions, like dreams, are unusual but quite natural occurrences which can be designated as "pathological" only when their morbid nature has been proved. From a strictly clinical standpoint Ezekiel's visions are of an archetypal nature and are not morbidly distorted in any way. There is no reason to regard them as pathological.[2] They are a symptom of the split which already existed at that time between conscious and unconscious. The first great vision is made up of two well-ordered compound quaternities, that is, conceptions of totality, such as we frequently observe today as spontaneous phenomena. Their *quinta essentia* is represented by a figure which has "the likeness of a human form."[3] Here Ezekiel has seen the essential content of the unconscious, namely *the idea of the higher man* by whom Yahweh was morally defeated and who he was later to become.

666   In India, a more or less simultaneous symptom of the same tendency was Gautama the Buddha (b. 562 B.C.), who gave the maximum differentiation of consciousness supremacy even over the highest Brahman gods. This development was a logical con-

---

[1] The vision in which he received his call occurred in 592 B.C.

[2] It is altogether wrong to assume that visions as such are pathological. They occur with normal people also—not very frequently, it is true, but they are by no means rare.

[3] Ezekiel 1 : 26.

sequence of the *purusha-atman* doctrine and derived from the inner experience of yoga practice.

667   Ezekiel grasped, in a symbol, the fact that Yahweh was drawing closer to man. This is something which came to Job as an experience but probably did not reach his consciousness. That is to say, he did not realize that his consciousness was higher than Yahweh's, and that consequently God wants to become man. What is more, in Ezekiel we meet for the first time the title "Son of Man," which Yahweh significantly uses in addressing the prophet, presumably to indicate that he is a son of the "Man" on the throne, and hence a prefiguration of the much later revelation in Christ. It is with the greatest right, therefore, that the four seraphim on God's throne became the emblems of the evangelists, for they form the quaternity which expresses Christ's totality, just as the four gospels represent the four pillars of his throne.

668   The disturbance of the unconscious continued for several centuries. Around 165 B.C., Daniel had a vision of four beasts and the "Ancient of Days," to whom "with the clouds of heaven there came one like a son of man." [4] Here the "son of man" is no longer the prophet but a son of the "Ancient of Days" in his own right, and a son whose task it is to rejuvenate the father.

669   The Book of Enoch, written around 100 B.C., goes into considerably more detail. It gives a revealing account of the advance of the sons of God into the world of men, another prefiguration which has been described as the "fall of the angels." Whereas, according to Genesis,[5] Yahweh resolved that his spirit should not "abide in man for ever," and that men should not live to be hundreds of years old as they had before, the sons of God, by way of compensation, fell in love with the beautiful daughters of men. This happened at the time of the giants. Enoch relates that after conspiring with one another, two hundred angels under the leadership of Samiazaz descended to earth, took the daughters of men to wife, and begat with them giants three thousand ells long.[6] The angels, among whom Azazel particularly excelled, taught mankind the arts and sciences. They proved to be extraordinarily progressive elements who broadened and developed man's consciousness, just as the wicked Cain had stood for progress as contrasted with the stay-at-home

4 Daniel 7:13.   5 Genesis 6:3f.   6 Enoch 7:2.

Abel. In this way they enlarged the significance of man to "gigantic" proportions, which points to an inflation of the cultural consciousness at that period. An inflation, however, is always threatened with a counter-stroke from the unconscious, and this actually did happen in the form of the Deluge. So corrupt was the earth before the Deluge that the giants "consumed all the acquisitions of men" and then began to devour each other, while men in their turn devoured the beasts, so that "the earth laid accusation against the lawless ones." [7]

670   The invasion of the human world by the sons of God therefore had serious consequences, which make Yahweh's precautions prior to his appearance on the earthly scene the more understandable. Man was completely helpless in face of this superior divine force. Hence it is of the greatest interest to see how Yahweh behaves in this matter. As the later Draconian punishment proves, it was a not unimportant event in the heavenly economy when no less than two hundred of the sons of God departed from the paternal household to carry out experiments on their own in the human world. One would have expected that information concerning this mass exodus would have trickled through to the court (quite apart from the fact of divine omniscience). But nothing of the sort happened. Only after the giants had long been begotten and had already started to slaughter and devour mankind did four archangels, apparently by accident, hear the weeping and wailing of men and discover what was going on on earth. One really does not know which is the more astonishing, the bad organization of the angelic hosts or the faulty communications in heaven. Be that as it may, this time the archangels felt impelled to appear before God with the following peroration:

All things are naked and open in Thy sight, and Thou seest all things, and nothing can hide itself from Thee. Thou seest what Azazel hath done, who taught all unrighteousness on earth and revealed the eternal secrets which were preserved in heaven. . . . [And enchantments hath Samiazaz taught], to whom Thou hast given authority to bear rule over his associates. . . . And Thou

[7] Enoch 7:3–6. [The translations of the Book of Enoch are from Charles, ed., *The Apocrypha and Pseudepigrapha of the Old Testament in English*, II, sometimes slightly modified.—TRANS.]

knowest all things before they come to pass, and Thou seest these things and Thou dost suffer them, and Thou dost not say to us what we are to do to them in regard to these.[8]

671 Either all that the archangels say is a lie, or Yahweh, for some incomprehensible reason, has drawn no conclusions from his omniscience, or—what is more likely—the archangels must remind him that once again he has preferred to know nothing of his omniscience. At any rate it is only on their intervention that retaliatory action is released on a global scale, but it is not really a just punishment, seeing that Yahweh promptly drowns all living creatures with the exception of Noah and his relatives. This intermezzo proves that the sons of God are somehow more vigilant, more progressive, and more conscious than their father. Yahweh's subsequent transformation is therefore to be rated all the higher. The preparations for his Incarnation give one the impression that he has really learnt something from experience and is setting about things more consciously than before. Undoubtedly the recollection of Sophia has contributed to this increase of consciousness. Parallel with this, the revelation of the metaphysical structure becomes more explicit. Whereas in Ezekiel and Daniel we find only vague hints about the quaternity and the Son of Man, Enoch gives us clear and detailed information on these points. The underworld, a sort of Hades, is divided into four hollow places which serve as abodes for the spirits of the dead until the Last Judgment. Three of these hollow places are dark, but one is bright and contains a "fountain of water." [9] This is the abode of the righteous.

672 With statements of this type we enter into a definitely psychological realm, namely that of mandala symbolism, to which also belong the ratios 1 : 3 and 3 : 4. The quadripartite Hades of Enoch corresponds to a chthonic quaternity, which presumably stands in everlasting contrast to a pneumatic or heavenly one. The former corresponds in alchemy to the *quaternio* of the elements, the latter to a fourfold, or total, aspect of the deity, as for instance Barbelo, Kolorbas, *Mercurius quadratus,* and the four-faced gods all indicate.

673 In fact, Enoch in his vision sees the four faces of God. Three

8 Enoch 9:5-11.   9 22:2.

of them are engaged in praising, praying, and supplicating, but the fourth in "fending off the Satans and forbidding them to come before the Lord of Spirits to accuse them who dwell on earth." [10]

674   The vision shows us an essential differentiation of the God-image: God now has four faces, or rather, four angels of his face, who are four hypostases or emanations, of which one is exclusively occupied in keeping his elder son Satan, now changed into many, away from him, and in preventing further experiments after the style of the Job episode.[11] The Satans still dwell in the heavenly regions, since the fall of Satan has not yet occurred. The above-mentioned proportions are also suggested here by the fact that three of the angels perform holy or beneficial functions, while the fourth is a militant figure who has to keep Satan at bay.

675   This quaternity has a distinctly pneumatic nature and is therefore expressed by angels, who are generally pictured with wings, i.e., as aerial beings. This is the more likely as they are presumably the descendants of Ezekiel's four seraphim.[12] The doubling and separation of the quaternity into an upper and a lower one, like the exclusion of the Satans from the heavenly court, points to a metaphysical split that had already taken place. But the pleromatic split is in its turn a symptom of a much deeper split in the divine will: the father wants to become the son, God wants to become man, the amoral wants to become exclusively good, the unconscious wants to become consciously responsible. So far everything exists only in statu nascendi.

676   Enoch's unconscious is vastly excited by all this and its contents burst out in a spate of apocalyptic visions. It also causes him to undertake the peregrinatio, the journey to the four quarters of heaven and to the centre of the earth, so that he draws a mandala with his own movements, in accordance with the "journeys" of the alchemistic philosophers and the corresponding fantasies of our modern unconscious.

677   When Yahweh addressed Ezekiel as "Son of Man," this was no more at first than a dark and enigmatic hint. But now it be-

10 Enoch 40 : 7.
11 Cf. also ch. 87f. Of the four "beings who were like white men," three take Enoch by the hand, while the other seizes a star and hurls it into the abyss.
12 Three had animal faces, one a human face.

comes clear: the man Enoch is not only the recipient of divine revelation but is at the same time a participant in the divine drama, as though he were at least one of the sons of God himself. This can only be taken as meaning that in the same measure as God sets out to become man, man is immersed in the pleromatic process. He becomes, as it were, baptized in it and is made to participate in the divine quaternity (i.e., is crucified with Christ). That is why even today, in the rite of the *benedictio fontis,* the water is divided into a cross by the hand of the priest and then sprinkled to the four quarters.

678   Enoch is so much under the influence of the divine drama, so gripped by it, that one could almost suppose he had a quite special understanding of the coming Incarnation. The "Son of Man" who is with the "Head [or Ancient] of Days" looks like an angel (i.e., like one of the sons of God). He "hath righteousness"; "with him dwelleth righteousness"; the Lord of Spirits has "chosen him"; "his lot hath the preeminence before the Lord of Spirits in uprightness." [13] It is probably no accident that so much stress is laid on righteousness, for it is the one quality that Yahweh lacks, a fact that could hardly have remained hidden from such a man as the author of the Book of Enoch. Under the reign of the Son of Man ". . . the prayer of the righteous has been heard, and the blood of the righteous . . . [avenged] before the Lord of Spirits." [14] Enoch sees a "fountain of righteousness which was inexhaustible." [15] The Son of Man

> . . . shall be a staff to the righteous. . . .
> For this reason hath he been chosen and hidden before
>   him,
> Before the creation of the world and for evermore.
> And the wisdom of the Lord of Spirits hath revealed
>   him . . . ,
> For he hath preserved the lot of the righteous.[16]
> For wisdom is poured out like water. . . .
> He is mighty in all the secrets of righteousness,
> And unrighteousness shall disappear as a shadow. . . .
> In him dwells the spirit of wisdom,

13 Enoch 46: 1–3.   14 47: 4.   15 48: 1.   16 48: 4, 6–7.

And the spirit which gives insight,
And the spirit of understanding and of might.[17]

679   Under the reign of the Son of Man

. . . shall the earth also give back that which has been
    entrusted to it,
And Sheol also shall give back that which it has received,
And hell [18] shall give back that which it owes. . . .

The Elect One shall in those days sit on My throne,
And his mouth shall pour forth all the secrets of
    wisdom and counsel.[19]

680   "All shall become angels in heaven." Azazel and his hosts
shall be cast into the burning fiery furnace for "becoming subject to Satan and leading astray those who dwell on the earth." [20]
681   At the end of the world the Son of Man shall sit in judgment
over all creatures. "The darkness shall be destroyed, and the
light established for ever." [21] Even Yahweh's two big exhibits,
Leviathan and Behemoth, are forced to succumb: they are
carved up and eaten. In this passage [22] Enoch is addressed by
the revealing angel with the title "Son of Man," a further indication that he, like Ezekiel, has been assimilated by the divine
mystery, is included in it, as is already suggested by the bare
fact that he witnesses it. Enoch is wafted away and takes his seat
in heaven. In the "heaven of heavens" he beholds the house of
God built of crystal, with streams of living fire about it, and
guarded by winged beings that never sleep.[23] The "Head of
Days" comes forth with the angelic quaternity (Michael, Ga-
briel, Raphael, Phanuel) and speaks to him, saying: "This is the
Son of Man who is born unto righteousness, and righteousness
abides over him, and the righteousness of the Head of Days for-
sakes him not." [24]
682   It is remarkable that the Son of Man and what he means
should be associated again and again with righteousness. It
seems to be his leitmotif, his chief concern. Only where injustice

17 Enoch 49 : 1–3.   18 Synonym for Sheol.   19 51 : 1, 3.
20 54 : 6. Here at last we hear that the exodus of the two hundred angels was a
prank of Satan's.
21 58 : 6 (mod.).   22 60 : 10.   23 71 : 5–6.   24 71 : 14.

threatens or has already occurred does such an emphasis on righteousness make any sense. No one, only God, can dispense justice to any noticeable degree, and precisely with regard to him there exists the justifiable fear that he may forget his justice. In this case his righteous son would intercede with him on man's behalf. Thus "the righteous shall have peace." [25] The justice that shall prevail under the son is stressed to such an extent that one has the impression that formerly, under the reign of the father, injustice was paramount, and that only with the son is the era of law and order inaugurated. It looks as though, with this, Enoch had unconsciously given an answer to Job.

683   The emphasis laid on God's agedness is logically connected with the existence of a son, but it also suggests that he himself will step a little into the background and leave the government of the human world more and more to the son, in the hope that a juster order will emerge. From all this we can see the after-effects of some psychological trauma, the memory of an injustice that cries to heaven and beclouds the intimate relationship with God. God himself wants a son, and man also wants a son to take the place of the father. This son must, as we have conclusively seen, be absolutely just, and this quality is given priority over all other virtues. God and man both want to escape from blind injustice.

684   Enoch, in his ecstasy, recognizes himself as the Son of Man, or as the son of God, although neither by birth nor by predestination does he seem to have been chosen for such a role.[26] He experiences that godlike elevation which, in the case of Job, we merely assumed, or rather inferred as the inevitable outcome. Job himself seems to have suspected something of the sort when he declares: "I know that my Vindicator lives." [27] This highly remarkable statement can, under the circumstances, only refer to the benevolent Yahweh. The traditional Christian interpretation of this passage as an anticipation of Christ is correct in so far as Yahweh's benevolent aspect incarnates itself, as its own hypostasis, in the Son of Man, and in so far as the Son of Man

---

25 71:17.
26 The author of the Book of Enoch chose, as the hero of his tale, Enoch the son of Jared, the seventh after Adam, who "walked with God," and, instead of dying, simply disappeared, i.e., was carried away by God (". . . and he was not, for God took him."—Genesis 5:24).   27 Job 19:25.

proves in Enoch to be a representative of justice and, in Christianity, the justifier of mankind. Furthermore, the Son of Man is pre-existent, and therefore Job could very well appeal to him. Just as Satan plays the role of accuser and slanderer, so Christ, God's other son, plays the role of advocate and defender.

685   Despite the contradiction, certain scholars have wished to see Enoch's Messianic ideas as Christian interpolations. For psychological reasons this suspicion seems to me unjustified. One has only to consider what Yahweh's injustice, his downright immorality, must have meant to a devout thinker. It was no laughing matter to be burdened with such an idea of God. A much later document tells us of a pious sage who could never read the Eighty-ninth Psalm, "because he could not bear it." When one considers with what intensity and exclusiveness not only Christ's teaching, but the doctrines of the Church in the following centuries down to the present day, have emphasized the goodness of the loving Father in heaven, the deliverance from fear, the Summum Bonum, and the *privatio boni,* one can form some conception of the incompatibility which the figure of Yahweh presents, and see how intolerable such a paradox must appear to the religious consciousness. And this has probably been so ever since the days of Job.

686   The inner instability of Yahweh is the prime cause not only of the creation of the world, but also of the pleromatic drama for which mankind serves as a tragic chorus. The encounter with the creature changes the creator. In the Old Testament writings we find increasing traces of this development from the sixth century B.C. on. The two main climaxes are formed firstly by the Job tragedy, and secondly by Ezekiel's revelation. Job is the innocent sufferer, but Ezekiel witnesses the humanization and differentiation of Yahweh. By being addressed as "Son of Man," it is intimated to him that Yahweh's incarnation and quaternity are, so to speak, the pleromatic model for what is going to happen, through the transformation and humanization of God, not only to God's son as foreseen from all eternity, but to man as such. This is fulfilled as an intuitive anticipation in Enoch. In his ecstasy he becomes the Son of Man in the pleroma, and his wafting away in a chariot (like Elijah) prefigures the resurrection of the dead. To fulfil his role as minister of justice he must get into immediate proximity to God, and as the pre-

existing Son of Man he is no longer subject to death. But in so far as he was an ordinary human being and therefore mortal, other mortals as well as he can attain to the vision of God; they too can become conscious of their saviour, and consequently immortal.

687   All these ideas could easily have become conscious at the time on the basis of the assumptions then current, if only someone had seriously reflected on them. For that no Christian interpolations were needed. The Book of Enoch was an anticipation in the grand manner, but everything still hung in mid air as mere revelation that never came down to earth. In view of these facts one cannot, with the best will in the world, see how Christianity, as we hear over and over again, is supposed to have burst upon world history as an absolute novelty. If ever anything had been historically prepared, and sustained and supported by the existing *Weltanschauung,* Christianity would be a classic example.

XII

688   Jesus first appears as a Jewish reformer and prophet of an exclusively good God. In so doing he saves the threatened religious continuity, and in this respect he does in fact prove himself a σωτήρ, a saviour. He preserves mankind from loss of communion with God and from getting lost in mere consciousness and rationality. That would have brought something like a dissociation between consciousness and the unconscious, an unnatural and even pathological condition, a "loss of soul" such as has threatened man from the beginning of time. Again and again and in increasing measure he gets into danger of overlooking the necessary irrationalities of his psyche, and of imagining that he can control everything by will and reason alone, and thus paddle his own canoe. This can be seen most clearly in the great socio-political movements, such as Socialism and Communism: under the former the state suffers, and under the latter, man.

689   Jesus, it is plain, translated the existing tradition into his own personal reality, announcing the glad tidings: "God has good pleasure in mankind. He is a loving father and loves you as I love you, and has sent me as his son to ransom you from the

old debt." He offers himself as an expiatory sacrifice that shall effect the reconciliation with God. The more desirable a real relationship of trust between man and God, the more astonishing becomes Yahweh's vindictiveness and irreconcilability towards his creatures. From a God who is a loving father, who is actually Love itself, one would expect understanding and forgiveness. So it comes as a nasty shock when this supremely good God only allows the purchase of such an act of grace through a human sacrifice, and, what is worse, through the killing of his own son. Christ apparently overlooked this anticlimax; at any rate all succeeding centuries have accepted it without opposition. One should keep before one's eyes the strange fact that the God of goodness is so unforgiving that he can only be appeased by a human sacrifice! This is an insufferable incongruity which modern man can no longer swallow, for he must be blind if he does not see the glaring light it throws on the divine character, giving the lie to all talk about love and the Summum Bonum.

690   Christ proves to be a mediator in two ways: he helps men against God and assuages the fear which man feels towards this being. He holds an important position midway between the two extremes, man and God, which are so difficult to unite. Clearly the focus of the divine drama shifts to the mediating God-man. He is lacking neither in humanity nor in divinity, and for this reason he was long ago characterized by totality symbols, because he was understood to be all-embracing and to unite all opposites. The quaternity of the Son of Man, indicating a more differentiated consciousness, was also ascribed to him (vide Cross and tetramorph). This corresponds by and large to the pattern in Enoch, but with one important deviation: Ezekiel and Enoch, the two bearers of the title "Son of Man," were ordinary human beings, whereas Christ by his descent,[1] conception, and birth is a hero and half-god in the classical sense. He is virginally begotten by the Holy Ghost and, as he is not a creaturely human being, has no inclination to sin. The infection of evil was in his case precluded by the preparations for the Incarnation. Christ therefore stands more on the divine than on the human level. He incarnates God's good will to the exclusion of all else and therefore does not stand exactly in the middle, because the essen-

[1] As a consequence of her immaculate conception Mary is already different from other mortals, and this fact is confirmed by her assumption.

tial thing about the creaturely human being, sin, does not touch him. Sin originally came from the heavenly court and entered into creation with the help of Satan, which enraged Yahweh to such an extent that in the end his own son had to be sacrificed in order to placate him. Strangely enough, he took no steps to remove Satan from his entourage. In Enoch a special archangel, Phanuel, was charged with the task of defending Yahweh from Satan's insinuations, and only at the end of the world shall Satan, in the shape of a star,[2] be bound hand and foot, cast into the abyss, and destroyed. (This is not the case in the Book of Revelation, where he remains eternally alive in his natural element.)

691 Although it is generally assumed that Christ's unique sacrifice broke the curse of original sin and finally placated God, Christ nevertheless seems to have had certain misgivings in this respect. What will happen to man, and especially to his own followers, when the sheep have lost their shepherd, and when they miss the one who interceded for them with the father? He assures his disciples that he will always be with them, nay more, that he himself abides within them. Nevertheless this does not seem to satisfy him completely, for in addition he promises to send them from the father another παράκλητος (advocate, "Counsellor"), in his stead, who will assist them by word and deed and remain with them forever.[3] One might conjecture from this that the "legal position" has still not been cleared up beyond a doubt, or that there still exists a factor of uncertainty.

692 The sending of the Paraclete has still another aspect. This Spirit of Truth and Wisdom is the Holy Ghost by whom Christ was begotten. He is the spirit of physical and spiritual procreation who from now on shall make his abode in creaturely man. Since he is the Third Person of the Deity, this is as much as to say that *God will be begotten in creaturely man.* This implies a tremendous change in man's status, for he is now raised to sonship and almost to the position of a man-god. With this the prefiguration in Ezekiel and Enoch, where, as we saw, the title "Son of Man" was already conferred on the creaturely man, is fulfilled. But that puts man, despite his continuing sinfulness, in

2 Presumably the "morning star" (cf. Revelation 2:28 and 22:16). This is the planet Venus in her psychological implications and not, as one might think, either of the two *malefici,* Saturn and Mars.   3 John 14:16.

the position of the mediator, the unifier of God and creature. Christ probably had this incalculable possibility in mind when he said: ". . . . he who believes in me, will also do the works that I do; and greater works than these will he do," [4] and, referring to the sixth verse of the Eighty-second Psalm, "I say, 'You are gods, sons of the Most High, all of you,' " he added, "and scripture cannot be broken." [5]

693   The future indwelling of the Holy Ghost in man amounts to a continuing incarnation of God. Christ, as the begotten son of God and pre-existing mediator, is a first-born and a divine paradigm which will be followed by further incarnations of the Holy Ghost in the empirical man. But man participates in the darkness of the world, and therefore, with Christ's death, a critical situation arises which might well be a cause for anxiety. When God became man all darkness and evil were carefully kept outside. Enoch's transformation into the Son of Man took place entirely in the realm of light, and to an even greater extent this is true of the incarnation in Christ. It is highly unlikely that the bond between God and man was broken with the death of Christ; on the contrary, the continuity of this bond is stressed again and again and is further confirmed by the sending of the Paraclete. But the closer this bond becomes, the closer becomes the danger of a collision with evil. On the basis of a belief that had existed quite early, the expectation grew up that the light manifestation would be followed by an equally dark one, and Christ by an Antichrist. Such an opinion is the last thing one would expect from the metaphysical situation, for the power of evil is supposedly overcome, and one can hardly believe that a loving father, after the whole complicated arrangement of salvation in Christ, the atonement and declaration of love for mankind, would again let loose his evil watch-dog on his children in complete disregard of all that had gone before. Why this wearisome forbearance towards Satan? Why this stubborn projection of evil on man, whom he has made so weak, so faltering, and so stupid that we are quite incapable of resisting his wicked sons? Why not pull up evil by the roots?

694   God, with his good intentions, begot a good and helpful son and thus created an image of himself as the good father—unfortunately, we must admit, again without considering that there

[4] John 14:12.   [5] 10:35.

existed in him a knowledge that spoke a very different truth. Had he only given an account of his action to himself, he would have seen what a fearful dissociation he had got into through his incarnation. Where, for instance, did his darkness go—that darkness by means of which Satan always manages to escape his well-earned punishment? Does he think he is completely changed and that his amorality has fallen from him? Even his "light" son, Christ, did not quite trust him in this respect. So now he sends to men the "spirit of truth," with whose help they will discover soon enough what happens when God incarnates only in his light aspect and believes he is goodness itself, or at least wants to be regarded as such. An enantiodromia in the grand style is to be expected. This may well be the meaning of the belief in the coming of the Antichrist, which we owe more than anything else to the activity of the "spirit of truth."

695   Although the Paraclete is of the greatest significance metaphysically, it was, from the point of view of the organization of the Church, most undesirable, because, as is authoritatively stated in scripture, the Holy Ghost is not subject to any control. In the interests of continuity and the Church the uniqueness of the incarnation and of Christ's work of redemption has to be strongly emphasized, and for the same reason the continuing indwelling of the Holy Ghost is discouraged and ignored as much as possible. No further individualistic digressions can be tolerated. Anyone who is inclined by the Holy Ghost towards dissident opinions necessarily becomes a heretic, whose persecution and elimination take a turn very much to Satan's liking. On the other hand one must realize that if everybody had tried to thrust the intuitions of his own private Holy Ghost upon others for the improvement of the universal doctrine, Christianity would rapidly have perished in a Babylonian confusion of tongues—a fate that lay threateningly close for many centuries.

696   It is the task of the Paraclete, the "spirit of truth," to dwell and work in individual human beings, so as to remind them of Christ's teachings and lead them into the light. A good example of this activity is Paul, who knew not the Lord and received his gospel not from the apostles but through revelation. He is one of those people whose unconscious was disturbed and produced revelatory ecstasies. The life of the Holy Ghost reveals itself through its own activity, and through effects which not

only confirm the things we all know, but go beyond them. In Christ's sayings there are already indications of ideas which go beyond the traditionally "Christian" morality—for instance the parable of the unjust steward, the moral of which agrees with the Logion of the Codex Bezae,[6] and betrays an ethical standard very different from what is expected. Here the moral criterion is *consciousness*, and not law or convention. One might also mention the strange fact that it is precisely Peter, who lacks self-control and is fickle in character, whom Christ wishes to make the rock and foundation of his Church. These seem to me to be ideas which point to the inclusion of evil in what I would call a *differential moral valuation*. For instance, it is good if evil is sensibly covered up, but to act unconsciously is evil. One might almost suppose that such views were intended for a time when consideration is given to evil as well as to good, or rather, when it is not suppressed below the threshold on the dubious assumption that we always know exactly what evil is.

697   Again, the expectation of the Antichrist is a far-reaching revelation or discovery, like the remarkable statement that despite his fall and exile the devil is still "prince of this world" and has his habitation in the all-surrounding air. In spite of his misdeeds and in spite of God's work of redemption for mankind, the devil still maintains a position of considerable power and holds all sublunary creatures under his sway. This situation can only be described as critical; at any rate it does not correspond to what could reasonably have been expected from the "glad tidings." Evil is by no means fettered, even though its days are numbered. God still hesitates to use force against Satan. Presumably he still does not know how much his own dark side favours the evil angel. Naturally this situation could not remain indefinitely hidden from the "spirit of truth" who has taken up his abode in man. He therefore created a disturbance in man's unconscious and produced, at the beginning of the Christian era, another great revelation which, because of its obscurity, gave rise to numerous interpretations and misinterpretations in the centuries that followed. This is the Revelation of St. John.

6 An apocryphal insertion at Luke 6:4. ["Man, if indeed thou knowest what thou doest, thou art blessed; but if thou knowest not, thou art cursed, and a transgressor of the law" (trans. in James, *The Apocryphal New Testament*, p. 33).—TRANS.]

XIII

698   One could hardly imagine a more suitable personality for
the John of the Apocalypse than the author of the Epistles of
John. It was he who declared that God is light and that "in him
is no darkness at all." [1] (Who said there was any darkness in
God?) Nevertheless, he knows that when we sin we need an
"advocate with the Father," and this is Christ, "the expiation
for our sins," [2] even though for his sake our sins are already for-
given. (Why then do we need an advocate?) The Father has be-
stowed his great love upon us (though it had to be bought at the
cost of a human sacrifice!), and we are the children of God. He
who is begotten by God commits no sin.[3] (Who commits *no* sin?)
John then preaches the message of love. God himself is love;
perfect love casteth out fear. But he must warn against false
prophets and teachers of false doctrines, and it is he who an-
nounces the coming of the Antichrist.[4] His conscious attitude is
orthodox, but he has evil forebodings. He might easily have
dreams that are not listed on his conscious programme. He talks
as if he knew not only a sinless state but also a perfect love,
unlike Paul, who was not lacking in the necessary self-reflection.
John is a bit too sure, and therefore he runs the risk of a dissociation. Under these circumstances a counterposition is bound to
grow up in the unconscious, which can then irrupt into consciousness in the form of a revelation. If this happens, the revelation will take the form of a more or less subjective myth, because,
among other things, it compensates the one-sidedness of an individual consciousness. This contrasts with the visions of Ezekiel
or Enoch, whose conscious situation was mainly characterized
by an ignorance (for which they were not to blame) and was
therefore compensated by a more or less objective and uni-
versally valid configuration of archetypal material.

699   So far as we can see, the Apocalypse conforms to these conditions. Even in the initial vision a fear-inspiring figure appears:
Christ blended with the Ancient of Days, having the likeness
of a man and the Son of Man. Out of his mouth goes a "sharp
two-edged sword," which would seem more suitable for fighting
and the shedding of blood than for demonstrating brotherly

1 I John 1:5.   2 2:1-2.   3 3:9.   4 2:18f., 4:3.

love. Since this Christ says to him, "Fear not," we must assume that John was not overcome by love when he fell "as though dead," [5] but rather by fear. (What price now the perfect love which casts out fear?)

700 Christ commands him to write seven epistles to the churches in the province of Asia. The church in Ephesus is admonished to repent; otherwise it is threatened with deprivation of the light ("I will come . . . and remove your candlestick from its place").[6] We also learn from this letter that Christ "hates" the Nicolaitans. (How does this square with love of your neighbour?)

701 The church in Smyrna does not come off so badly. Its enemies supposedly are Jews, but they are "a synagogue of Satan," which does not sound too friendly.

702 Pergamum is censured because a teacher of false doctrines is making himself conspicuous there, and the place swarms with Nicolaitans. Therefore it must repent—"if not, I will come to you soon." This can only be interpreted as a threat.

703 Thyatira tolerates the preaching of "that woman Jezebel, who calls herself a prophetess." He will "throw her on a sickbed" and "strike her children dead." But "he who . . . keeps my works until the end, I will give him power over the nations, and he shall rule them with a rod of iron, as when earthen pots are broken in pieces, even as I myself have received power from my Father; and I will give him the morning star." [7] Christ, as we know, teaches "Love your enemies," but here he threatens a massacre of children all too reminiscent of Bethlehem!

704 The works of the church in Sardis are not perfect before God. Therefore, "repent." Otherwise he will come like a thief, "and you will not know at what hour I will come upon you" [8]—a none too friendly warning.

705 In regard to Philadelphia, there is nothing to be censured. But Laodicea he will spew out of his mouth, because they are lukewarm. They too must repent. His explanation is characteristic: "Those whom I love, I reprove and chasten." [9] It would be quite understandable if the Laodiceans did not want too much of this "love."

706 Five of the seven churches get bad reports. This apocalyptic "Christ" behaves rather like a bad-tempered, power-conscious

[5] Cf. Rev. 1 : 16–17.　　[6] Rev. 2 : 5.　　[7] 2 : 20f.　　[8] 3 : 3.　　[9] 3 : 19.

"boss" who very much resembles the "shadow" of a love-preaching bishop.

707   As if in confirmation of what I have said, there now follows a vision in the style of Ezekiel. But he who sat upon the throne did not look like a man, but was to look upon "like jasper and carnelian." [10] Before him was "a sea of glass, like crystal"; around the throne, four "living creatures" (ζῷα), which were "full of eyes in front and behind . . . all round and within." [11] The symbol of Ezekiel appears here strangely modified: stone, glass, crystal—dead and rigid things deriving from the inorganic realm—characterize the Deity. One is inevitably reminded of the preoccupation of the alchemists during the following centuries, when the mysterious "Man," the *homo altus*, was named λίθος οὐ λίθος, 'the stone that is no stone,' and multiple eyes gleamed in the ocean of the unconscious.[12] At any rate, something of John's psychology comes in here, which has caught a glimpse of things beyond the Christian cosmos.

708   Hereupon follows the opening of the Book with Seven Seals by the "Lamb." The latter has put off the human features of the "Ancient of Days" and now appears in purely theriomorphic but monstrous form, like one of the many other horned animals in the Book of Revelation. It has seven eyes and seven horns, and is therefore more like a ram than a lamb. Altogether it must have looked pretty awful. Although it is described as "standing, as though it had been slain," [13] it does not behave at all like an innocent victim, but in a very lively manner indeed. From the first four seals it lets loose the four sinister apocalyptic horsemen. With the opening of the fifth seal, we hear the martyrs crying for vengeance ("O sovereign Lord, holy and true, how long before thou wilt judge and avenge our blood on those who dwell upon the earth?").[14] The sixth seal brings a cosmic catastrophe, and everything hides from the "wrath of the Lamb," "for the great day of his wrath is come." [15] We no longer recognize the meek Lamb who lets himself be led unresistingly to the slaughter; there is only the aggressive and irascible ram whose rage can at last be vented. In all this I see less a metaphysical

---

[10] 4 : 3.   [11] 4 : 6f.
[12] This refers to the "luminosity" of the archetypes. [Cf. Jung, "On the Nature of the Psyche," pars. 388ff.—EDITORS.]
[13] Rev. 5 : 6.   [14] 6 : 10.   [15] 6 : 17 (AV).

mystery than the outburst of long pent-up negative feelings such as can frequently be observed in people who strive for perfection. We can take it as certain that the author of the Epistles of John made every effort to practise what he preached to his fellow Christians. For this purpose he had to shut out all negative feelings, and, thanks to a helpful lack of self-reflection, he was able to forget them. But though they disappeared from the conscious level they continued to rankle beneath the surface, and in the course of time spun an elaborate web of resentments and vengeful thoughts which then burst upon consciousness in the form of a revelation. From this there grew up a terrifying picture that blatantly contradicts all ideas of Christian humility, tolerance, love of your neighbour and your enemies, and makes nonsense of a loving father in heaven and rescuer of mankind. A veritable orgy of hatred, wrath, vindictiveness, and blind destructive fury that revels in fantastic images of terror breaks out and with blood and fire overwhelms a world which Christ had just endeavoured to restore to the original state of innocence and loving communion with God.

709   The opening of the seventh seal naturally brings a new flood of miseries which threaten to exhaust even St. John's unholy imagination. As if to fortify himself, he must now eat a "little scroll" in order to go on with his "prophesying."

710   When the seventh angel had finally ceased blowing his trumpet, there appeared in heaven, after the destruction of Jerusalem, a vision of the *sun-woman*, "with the moon under her feet, and on her head a crown of twelve stars." [16] She was in the pangs of birth, and before her stood a great red dragon that wanted to devour her child.

711   This vision is altogether out of context. Whereas with the previous visions one has the impression that they were afterwards revised, rearranged, and embellished, one feels that this image is original and not intended for any educational purpose. The vision is introduced by the opening of the temple in heaven and the sight of the Ark of the Covenant. [17] This is probably a prelude to the descent of the heavenly bride, Jerusalem, an equivalent of Sophia, for it is all part of the heavenly *hieros gamos*, whose fruit is a divine man-child. He is threatened with the fate of Apollo, the son of Leto, who was likewise pursued

16 Rev. 12:1.   17 Rev. 11:19. The *arca foederis* is an *allegoria Mariae*.

by a dragon. But here we must dwell for a moment on the figure
of the mother. She is "a woman clothed with the sun." Note the
simple statement "a woman"—an ordinary woman, not a goddess
and not an eternal virgin immaculately conceived. No special
precautions exempting her from complete womanhood are
noticeable, except the cosmic and naturalistic attributes which
mark her as an *anima mundi* and peer of the primordial cosmic
man, or Anthropos. She is the feminine Anthropos, the counterpart of the masculine principle. The pagan Leto motif is eminently suited to illustrate this, for in Greek mythology matri-
archal and patriarchal elements are about equally mixed. The
stars above, the moon below, in the middle the sun, the rising
Horus and the setting Osiris, and the maternal night all round,
οὐρανὸς ἄνω, οὐρανὸς κάτω[18]—this symbolism reveals the whole mystery of the "woman": she contains in her darkness the sun of
"masculine" consciousness, which rises as a child out of the noc-
turnal sea of the unconscious, and as an old man sinks into it
again. She adds the dark to the light, symbolizes the hierogamy
of opposites, and reconciles nature with spirit.

712   The son who is born of these heavenly nuptials is perforce a
complexio oppositorum, a uniting symbol, a totality of life.
John's unconscious, certainly not without reason, borrowed
from Greek mythology in order to describe this strange eschatological experience, for it was not on any account to be confused
with the birth of the Christ-child which had occurred long before under quite different circumstances. Though obviously the
allusion is to the "wrathful Lamb," i.e., the apocalyptic Christ,
the new-born man-child is represented as his duplicate, as one
who will "rule the nations with a rod of iron."[19] He is thus
assimilated to the predominant feelings of hatred and vengeance, so that it looks as if he will needlessly continue to wreak
his judgment even in the distant future. This interpretation
does not seem consistent, because the Lamb is already charged
with this task and, in the course of the revelation, carries it to
an end without the newborn man-child ever having an opportunity to act on his own. He never reappears afterwards. I am
therefore inclined to believe that the depiction of him as a son
of vengeance, if it is not an interpretative interpolation, must
have been a familiar phrase to John and that it slipped out as

[18] "Heaven above, heaven below."   [19] Rev. 12:5; cf. 2:27.

77

the obvious interpretation. This is the more probable in that the intermezzo could not at the time have been understood in any other way, even though this interpretation is quite meaningless. As I have already pointed out, the sun-woman episode is a foreign body in the flow of the visions. Therefore, I believe, it is not too far-fetched to conjecture that the author of the Apocalypse, or perhaps a perplexed transcriber, felt the need to interpret this obvious parallel with Christ and somehow bring it into line with the text as a whole. This could easily be done by using the familiar image of the shepherd with the iron crook. I cannot see any other reason for this association.

713   The man-child is "caught up" to God, who is manifestly his father, and the mother is hidden in the wilderness. This would seem to indicate that the child-figure will remain latent for an indefinite time and that its activity is reserved for the future. The story of Hagar may be a prefiguration of this. The similarity between this story and the birth of Christ obviously means no more than that the birth of the man-child is an analogous event, like the previously mentioned enthronement of the Lamb in all his metaphysical glory, which must have taken place long before at the time of the ascension. In the same way the dragon, i.e., the devil, is described as being thrown down to earth,[20] although Christ had already observed the fall of Satan very much earlier. This strange repetition or duplication of the characteristic events in Christ's life gave rise to the conjecture that a second Messiah is to be expected at the end of the world. What is meant here cannot be the return of Christ himself, for we are told that he would come "in the clouds of heaven," but not be *born* a second time, and certainly not from a sun-moon conjunction. The epiphany at the end of the world corresponds more to the content of Revelation 1 and 19:11ff. The fact that John uses the myth of Leto and Apollo in describing the birth may be an indication that the vision, in contrast to the Christian tradition, is a product of the unconscious.[21] But in the unconscious is everything that has been rejected by consciousness, and the more Christian one's consciousness is, the more heathenishly does the

[20] Rev. 12:9.
[21] It is very probable that John knew the Leto myth and used it consciously. What was unconscious and most unexpected, however, was the fact that his unconscious used this pagan myth to describe the birth of the second Messiah.

unconscious behave, if in the rejected heathenism there are values which are important for life—if, that is to say, the baby has been thrown out with the bath water, as so often happens. The unconscious does not isolate or differentiate its objects as consciousness does. It does not think abstractly or apart from the subject: the person of the ecstatic or visionary is always drawn into the process and included in it. In this case it is John himself whose unconscious personality is more or less identified with Christ; that is to say, he is born like Christ, and born to a like destiny. John is so completely captivated by the archetype of the divine son that he sees its activity in the unconscious; in other words, he sees how God is born again in the (partly pagan) unconscious, indistinguishable from the self of John, since the "divine child" is a symbol of the one as much as the other, just as Christ is. Consciously, of course, John was very far from thinking of Christ as a symbol. For the believing Christian, Christ is everything, but certainly not a symbol, which is an expression for something unknown or not yet knowable. And yet he is a symbol by his very nature. Christ would never have made the impression he did on his followers if he had not expressed something that was alive and at work in their unconscious. Christianity itself would never have spread through the pagan world with such astonishing rapidity had its ideas not found an analogous psychic readiness to receive them. It is this fact which also makes it possible to say that whoever believes in Christ is not only contained in him, but that Christ then dwells in the believer as the perfect man formed in the image of God, the second Adam. Psychologically, it is the same relationship as that in Indian philosophy between man's ego-consciousness and *purusha*, or *atman*. It is the ascendency of the "complete"—τέλειος—or total human being, consisting of the totality of the psyche, of conscious and unconscious, over the ego, which represents only consciousness and its contents and knows nothing of the unconscious, although in many respects it is dependent on the unconscious and is often decisively influenced by it. This relationship of the self to the ego is reflected in the relationship of Christ to man. Hence the unmistakable analogies between certain Indian and Christian ideas, which have given rise to conjectures of Indian influence on Christianity.

714   This parallelism, which has so far remained latent in John,

now bursts into consciousness in the form of a vision. That this invasion is authentic can be seen from the use of pagan mythological material, a most improbable procedure for a Christian of that time, especially as it contains traces of astrological influence. That may explain the thoroughly pagan remark, "And the earth helped the woman." [22] Even though the consciousness of that age was exclusively filled with Christian ideas, earlier or contemporaneous pagan contents lay just below the surface, as for example in the case of St. Perpetua.[23] With a Judaeo-Christian—and the author of the Apocalypse was probably such—another possible model to be considered is the cosmic Sophia, to whom John refers on more than one occasion. She could easily be taken as the mother of the divine child,[24] since she is obviously a woman in heaven, i.e., a goddess or consort of a god. Sophia comes up to this definition, and so does the transfigured Mary. If the vision were a modern dream one would not hesitate to interpret the birth of the divine child as the coming to consciousness of the self. In John's case the conscious attitude of faith made it possible for the Christ-image to be received into the material of the unconscious; it activated the archetype of the divine virgin mother and of the birth of her son-lover, and brought it face to face with his Christian consciousness. As a result, John became personally involved in the divine drama.

715   His Christ-image, clouded by negative feelings, has turned into a savage avenger who no longer bears any real resemblance to a saviour. One is not at all sure whether this Christ-figure may not in the end have more of the human John in it, with his compensating shadow, than of the divine saviour who, as the *lumen de lumine,* contains "no darkness." The grotesque paradox of the "wrathful Lamb" should have been enough to arouse our suspicions in this respect. We can turn and twist it as we like, but, seen in the light of the gospel of love, the avenger and judge remains a most sinister figure. This, one suspects, may have been the reason which moved John to assimilate the new-born man-child to the figure of the avenger, thereby blurring his mythological character as the lovely and lovable divine youth

---

22 Rev. 12 : 16 (AV).
23 [Cf. Marie-Louise von Franz, "Die Passio Perpetuae."—EDITORS.]
24 The son would then correspond to the *filius sapientiae* of medieval alchemy.

whom we know so well in the figures of Tammuz, Adonis, and Balder. The enchanting springlike beauty of this divine youth is one of those pagan values which we miss so sorely in Christianity, and particularly in the sombre world of the apocalypse— the indescribable morning glory of a day in spring, which after the deathly stillness of winter causes the earth to put forth and blossom, gladdens the heart of man and makes him believe in a kind and loving God.

716 As a totality, the self is by definition always a *complexio oppositorum,* and the more consciousness insists on its own luminous nature and lays claim to moral authority, the more the self will appear as something dark and menacing. We may assume such a condition in John, since he was a shepherd of his flock and also a fallible human being. Had the apocalypse been a more or less personal affair of John's, and hence nothing but an outburst of personal resentment, the figure of the wrathful Lamb would have satisfied this need completely. Under those conditions the new-born man-child would have been bound to have a noticeably positive aspect, because, in accordance with his symbolic nature, he would have compensated the intolerable devastation wrought by the outburst of long pent-up passions, being the child of the conjunction of opposites, of the sunfilled day world and the moonlit night world. He would have acted as a mediator between the loving and the vengeful sides of John's nature, and would thus have become a beneficent saviour who restored the balance. This positive aspect, however, must have escaped John's notice, otherwise he could never have conceived of the child as standing on the same level as the avenging Christ.

717 But John's problem was not a personal one. It was not a question of his personal unconscious or of an outburst of ill humour, but of visions which came up from a far greater and more comprehensive depth, namely from the collective unconscious. His problem expresses itself far too much in collective and archetypal forms for us to reduce it to a merely personal situation. To do so would be altogether too easy as well as being wrong in theory and practice. As a Christian, John was seized by a collective, archetypal process, and he must therefore be explained first and foremost in that light. He certainly also had his personal psychology, into which we, if we may regard the

81

author of the Epistles and the apocalyptist as one and the same person, have some insight. That the imitation of Christ creates a corresponding shadow in the unconscious hardly needs demonstrating. The fact that John had visions at all is evidence of an unusual tension between conscious and unconscious. If he is identical with the author of the Epistles, he must have been quite old when he wrote the Book of Revelation. *In confinio mortis* and in the evening of a long and eventful life a man will often see immense vistas of time stretching out before him. Such a man no longer lives in the everyday world and in the vicissitudes of personal relationships, but in the sight of many aeons and in the movement of ideas as they pass from century to century. The eye of John penetrates into the distant future of the Christian aeon and into the dark abyss of those forces which his Christianity kept in equilibrium. What burst upon him is the storm of the times, the premonition of a tremendous enantiodromia which he could only understand as the final annihilation of the darkness which had not comprehended the light that appeared in Christ. He failed to see that the power of destruction and vengeance is that very darkness from which God had split himself off when he became man. Therefore he could not understand, either, what that sun-moon-child meant, and he could only interpret it as another figure of vengeance. The passion that breaks through in his revelation bears no trace of the feebleness or serenity of old age, because it is infinitely more than personal resentment: it is the spirit of God itself, which blows through the weak mortal frame and again demands man's *fear* of the unfathomable Godhead.

XIV

718   The torrent of negative feelings seems to be inexhaustible, and the dire events continue their course. Out of the sea come monsters "with horns" (i.e., endowed with power), the horrid progeny of the deep. Faced with all this darkness and destruction, man's terrified consciousness quite understandably looks round for a mountain of refuge, an island of peace and safety. John therefore weaves in a vision of the Lamb on Mount Zion, where the hundred and forty-four thousand elect and redeemed

are gathered round the Lamb.[1] They are the παρθένοι, the male virgins, "which were not defiled with women."[2] They are the ones who, following in the footsteps of the young dying god, have never become complete human beings, but have voluntarily renounced their share in the human lot and have said no to the continuance of life on earth.[3] If everyone were converted to this point of view, man as a species would die out in a few decades. But of such preordained ones there are relatively few. John believed in predestination in accordance with higher authority. This is rank pessimism.

> Everything created
> Is worth being liquidated

says Mephisto.

719   This only moderately comforting prospect is immediately interrupted by the warning angels. The first angel proclaims an "everlasting gospel," the quintessence of which is "Fear God!" There is no more talk of God's love. What is feared can only be something fearful.[4]

720   The Son of Man now appears holding a sharp sickle in his hand, together with an auxiliary angel who also has a sickle.[5] But the grape harvest consists in an unparalleled blood-bath: the angel "gathered the vintage of the earth, and threw it into the great winepress of the wrath of God . . . and blood flowed from the winepress"—in which human beings were trodden!— "as high as a horse's bridle, for one thousand six hundred stadia."[6]

721   Seven angels then come out of the heavenly temple with the seven vials of wrath, which they proceed to pour out on the earth.[7] The *pièce de résistance* is the destruction of the Great

1 Rev. 14:1. It may be significant that there is no longer any talk of the "great multitude which no man could number, from every nation, from all tribes and peoples and tongues, standing before the throne and before the Lamb," who were mentioned in 7:9.   2 14:4 (AV).

3 They really belong to the cult of the Great Mother, since they correspond to the emasculated Galli. Cf. the strange passage in Matthew 19:12, about the eunuchs "who have made themselves eunuchs for the sake of the kingdom of heaven," like the priests of Cybele who used to castrate themselves in honour of her son Attis.   4 Cf. also Rev. 19:5.

5 14:14 and 17. The auxiliary angel might well be John himself.

6 14:19–20.   7 15:6–7 and 16:1ff.

Whore of Babylon, the counterpart of the heavenly Jerusalem. The Whore is the chthonic equivalent of the sun-woman Sophia, with, however, a reversal in moral character. If the elect turn themselves into "virgins" in honour of the Great Mother Sophia, a gruesome fantasy of fornication is spawned in the unconscious by way of compensation. The destruction of Babylon therefore represents not only the end of fornication, but the utter eradication of all life's joys and pleasures, as can be seen from 18:22–23:

> and the sound of harpers and minstrels, of flute players
>   and trumpeters,
>   shall be heard in thee no more;
>
>   . . . .
>
> and the light of a lamp
>   shall shine in thee no more;
> and the voice of bridegroom and bride
>   shall be heard in thee no more . . .

722   As we happen to be living at the end of the Christian aeon Pisces, one cannot help but recall the doom that has overtaken our modern art.

723   Symbols like Jerusalem, Babylon, etc. are always overdetermined, that is, they have several aspects of meaning and can therefore be interpreted in different ways. I am only concerned with the psychological aspect, and do not wish to express an opinion as to their possible connection with historical events.

724   The destruction of all beauty and of all life's joys, the unspeakable suffering of the whole of creation that once sprang from the hand of a lavish Creator, would be, for a feeling heart, an occasion for deepest melancholy. But John cries: "Rejoice over her, thou heaven, ye holy apostles and prophets, for God hath avenged you on her [Babylon]," [8] from which we can see how far vindictiveness and lust for destruction can go, and what the "thorn in the flesh" means.

725   It is Christ who, leading the hosts of angels, treads "the winepress of the fierceness and wrath of Almighty God." [9] His robe "is dipped in blood." [10] He rides a *white horse*,[11] and with the

---

[8] Rev. 18:20 (AV).   [9] 19:15 (AV).   [10] 19:13.

[11] 19:11. Here again astrological speculations concerning the second half of the Christian aeon may be implied, with Pegasus as paranatellon of Aquarius.

sword which issues out of his mouth he kills the beast and the "false prophet," presumably his—or John's—dark counterpart, i.e., the shadow. Satan is locked up in the bottomless pit for a thousand years, and *Christ shall reign for the same length of time*. "After that he must be loosed a little season." [12] These thousand years correspond astrologically to the first half of the Pisces aeon. The setting free of Satan after this time must therefore correspond—one cannot imagine any other reason for it— to the enantiodromia of the Christian aeon, that is, to the reign of the Antichrist, whose coming could be predicted on astrological grounds. Finally, at the end of an unspecified period, the devil is thrown into the lake of fire and brimstone for ever and ever (but not completely destroyed as in Enoch), and the whole of the first creation disappears. [13]

726   The *hieros gamos,* the marriage of the Lamb with "his Bride," which had been announced earlier, [14] can now take place. The bride is the "new Jerusalem coming down out of heaven." [15] Her "radiance [was] like a most rare jewel, like a jasper, clear as crystal." [16] The city was built foursquare and was of pure gold, clear as glass, and so were its streets. The Lord God himself and the Lamb are its temple, and the source of never-ending light. There is no night in the city, and nothing unclean can enter into defile it. [17] (This repeated assurance allays a doubt in John that has never been quite silenced.) From the throne of God and the Lamb flows the river of the water of life, and beside it stands the tree of life, as a reminder of paradise and pleromatic pre-existence. [18]

727   This final vision, which is generally interpreted as referring to the relationship of Christ to his Church, has the meaning of a "uniting symbol" and is therefore a representation of perfection and wholeness: hence the quaternity, which expresses itself in the city as a quadrangle, in paradise as the four rivers, in Christ as the four evangelists, and in God as the four living creatures. While the circle signifies the roundness of heaven and the all-embracing nature of the "pneumatic" deity, the square refers to the earth. [19] Heaven is masculine, but the earth is feminine. Therefore God has his throne in heaven, while Wisdom

---

[12] Rev. 20:3 (AV).   [13] 20:10 and 21:1.   [14] 19:7.   [15] 21:2.
[16] 21:11.   [17] 21:16–27.   [18] 22:1–2.
[19] In China, heaven is round and the earth square.

has hers on the earth, as she says in Ecclesiasticus: "Likewise in the beloved city he gave me rest, and in Jerusalem was my power." She is the "mother of fair love," [20] and when John pictures Jerusalem as the bride he is probably following Ecclesiasticus. The city is Sophia, who was with God before time began, and at the end of time will be reunited with God through the sacred marriage. As a feminine being she coincides with the earth, from which, so a Church Father tells us, Christ was born,[21] and hence with the quaternity of the four living creatures in whom God manifests himself in Ezekiel. In the same way that Sophia signifies God's self-reflection, the four seraphim represent God's consciousness with its four functional aspects. The many perceiving eyes [22] which are concentrated in the four wheels point in the same direction. They represent a fourfold synthesis of unconscious luminosities, corresponding to the tetrameria of the *lapis philosophorum,* of which the description of the heavenly city reminds us: everything sparkles with precious gems, crystal, and glass, in complete accordance with Ezekiel's vision of God. And just as the *hieros gamos* unites Yahweh with Sophia (Shekinah in the Cabala), thus restoring the original pleromatic state, so the parallel description of God and city points to their common nature: they are originally one, a single hermaphroditic being, an archetype of the greatest universality.

728   No doubt this is meant as a final solution of the terrible conflict of existence. The solution, however, as here presented, does not consist in the reconciliation of the opposites, but in their final severance, by which means those whose destiny it is to be saved can save themselves by identifying with the bright pneumatic side of God. An indispensable condition for this seems to be the denial of propagation and of sexual life altogether.

20 Ecclesiasticus 24:11 and 18 (AV).

21 Tertullian, *Adversus Judaeos,* XIII (Migne, *P.L.,* vol. 2, col. 635): ". . . . illa terra virgo nondum pluviis rigata nec imbribus foecundata, ex qua homo tunc primum plasmatus est, ex qua nunc Christus secundum carnem ex virgine natus est" (. . . that virgin soil, not yet watered by the rains nor fertilized by the showers, from which man was originally formed [and] from which Christ is now born of a Virgin through the flesh).

22 Ezekiel 1:18.

XV

729   The Book of Revelation is on the one hand so personal and on the other so archetypal and collective that one is obliged to consider both aspects. Our modern interest would certainly turn first to the person of John. As I have said before, it is possible that John the author of the Epistles is identical with the apocalyptist. The psychological findings speak in favour of such an assumption. The "revelation" was experienced by an early Christian who, as a leading light of the community, presumably had to live an exemplary life and demonstrate to his flock the Christian virtues of true faith, humility, patience, devotion, selfless love, and denial of all worldly desires. In the long run this can become too much, even for the most righteous. Irritability, bad moods, and outbursts of affect are the classic symptoms of chronic virtuousness.[1] In regard to his Christian attitude, his own words probably give us the best picture:

> Beloved, let us love one another; for love is of God, and he who loves is born of God and knows God. He who does not love does not know God; for God is love. . . . In this is love, not that we loved God but that he loved us and sent his Son to be the expiation for our sins. Beloved, if God so loved us, we also ought to love one another. . . . So we know and believe the love God has for us. God is love, and he who abides in love abides in God, and God abides in him. . . . There is no fear in love, but perfect love casts out fear. For fear has to do with punishment, and he who fears is not perfected in love. . . . If any one says, "I love God," and hates his brother, he is a liar; for he who does not love his brother whom he has seen, cannot love God whom he has not seen. And this commandment we have from him, that he who loves God should love his brother also.[2]

730   But who hates the Nicolaitans? Who thirsts for vengeance and even wants to throw "that woman Jezebel" on a sickbed and strike her children dead? Who cannot have enough of bloodthirsty fantasies? Let us be psychologically correct, however: it is not the conscious mind of John that thinks up these fantasies,

---

1 Not for nothing was the apostle John nicknamed "son of thunder" by Christ.
2 I John 4 : 7–21.

they come to him in a violent "revelation." They fall upon him involuntarily with an unexpected vehemence and with an intensity which, as said, far transcends anything we could expect as compensation of a somewhat one-sided attitude of consciousness.

731   I have seen many compensating dreams of believing Christians who deceived themselves about their real psychic constitution and imagined that they were in a different condition from what they were in reality. But I have seen nothing that even remotely resembles the brutal impact with which the opposites collide in John's visions, except in the case of severe psychosis. However, John gives us no grounds for such a diagnosis. His apocalyptic visions are not confused enough; they are too consistent, not subjective and scurrilous enough. Considering the nature of their subject, the accompanying affects are adequate. Their author need not necessarily be an unbalanced psychopath. It is sufficient that he is a passionately religious person with an otherwise well-ordered psyche. But he must have an intensive relationship to God which lays him open to an invasion far transcending anything personal. The really religious person, in whom the capacity for an unusual extension of consciousness is inborn, must be prepared for such dangers.

732   The purpose of the apocalyptic visions is not to tell John, as an ordinary human being, how much shadow he hides beneath his luminous nature, but to open the seer's eye to the immensity of God, for he who loves God will know God. We can say that just because John loved God and did his best to love his fellows also, this "gnosis," this knowledge of God, struck him. Like Job, he saw the fierce and terrible side of Yahweh. For this reason he felt his gospel of love to be one-sided, and he supplemented it with the gospel of fear: *God can be loved but must be feared.*

733   With this, the seer's range of vision extends far beyond the first half of the Christian aeon: he divines that the reign of Antichrist will begin after a thousand years, a clear indication that Christ was not an unqualified victor. John anticipated the alchemists and Jakob Böhme; maybe he even sensed his own personal implication in the divine drama, since he anticipated the possibility of God's birth in man, which the alchemists, Meister Eckhart, and Angelus Silesius also intuited. He thus outlined the programme for the whole aeon of Pisces, with its

dramatic enantiodromia, and its dark end which we have still to experience, and before whose—without exaggeration—truly apocalyptic possibilities mankind shudders. The four sinister horsemen, the threatening tumult of trumpets, and the brimming vials of wrath are still waiting; already the atom bomb hangs over us like the sword of Damocles, and behind that lurk the incomparably more terrible possibilities of chemical warfare, which would eclipse even the horrors described in the Apocalypse. *Luciferi vires accendit Aquarius acres*—"Aquarius sets aflame Lucifer's harsh forces." Could anyone in his right senses deny that John correctly foresaw at least some of the possible dangers which threaten our world in the final phase of the Christian aeon? He knew, also, that the fire in which the devil is tormented burns in the divine pleroma for ever. God has a terrible double aspect: a sea of grace is met by a seething lake of fire, and the light of love glows with a fierce dark heat of which it is said "ardet non lucet"—it burns but gives no light. That is the eternal, as distinct from the temporal, gospel: *one can love God but must fear him.*

XVI

734   The book of Revelation, rightly placed at the end of the New Testament, reaches beyond it into a future that is all too palpably close with its apocalyptic terrors. The decision of an ill-considered moment, made in some Herostratic head,[1] can suffice to unleash the world cataclysm. The thread by which our fate hangs is wearing thin. Not nature, but the "genius of mankind," has knotted the hangman's noose with which it can execute itself at any moment. This is simply another *façon de parler* for what John called the "wrath of God."

735   Unfortunately we have no means of envisaging how John— if, as I surmise, he is the same as the author of the Epistles— would have come to terms with the double aspect of God. It is possible, even probable, that he was not aware of any contrast. It is altogether amazing how little most people reflect on numinous objects and attempt to come to terms with them, and

1 [Herostratus, in order to make his name immortal, burned down the temple of Artemis in Ephesus, in 365 B.C.—EDITORS.]

ɔw laborious such an undertaking is once we have embarked pon it. The numinosity of the object makes it difficult to handle intellectually, since our affectivity is always involved. One always participates for or against, and "absolute objectivity" is more rarely achieved here than anywhere else. If one has positive religious convictions, i.e., if one believes, then doubt is felt as very disagreeable and also one fears it. For this reason, one prefers not to analyse the object of belief. If one has no religious beliefs, then one does not like to admit the feeling of deficit, but prates loudly about one's liberal-mindedness and pats oneself on the back for the noble frankness of one's agnosticism. From this standpoint, it is hardly possible to admit the numinosity of the religious object, and yet its very numinosity is just as great a hindrance to critical thinking, because the unpleasant possibility might then arise that one's faith in enlightenment or agnosticism would be shaken. Both types feel, without knowing it, the insufficiency of their argument. Enlightenment operates with an inadequate rationalistic concept of truth and points triumphantly to the fact that beliefs such as the virgin birth, divine filiation, the resurrection of the dead, transubstantiation, etc., are all moonshine. Agnosticism maintains that it does not possess any knowledge of God or of anything metaphysical, overlooking the fact that one never *possesses* a metaphysical belief but is *possessed by it*. Both are possessed by reason, which represents the supreme arbiter who cannot be argued with. But who or what is this "reason" and why should it be supreme? Is not something that *is* and has real existence for us an authority superior to any rational judgment, as has been shown over and over again in the history of the human mind? Unfortunately the defenders of "faith" operate with the same futile arguments, only the other way about. The only thing which is beyond doubt is that there are metaphysical statements which are asserted or denied with considerable affect precisely because of their numinosity. This fact gives us a sure empirical basis from which to proceed. It is objectively real as a psychic phenomenon. The same applies naturally to all statements, even the most contradictory, that ever were or still are numinous. From now on we shall have to consider religious statements in their totality.

XVII

736 Let us turn back to the question of coming to terms with
the paradoxical idea of God which the Apocalypse reveals to us.
Evangelical Christianity, in the strict sense, has no need to
bother with it, because it has as an essential doctrine an idea of
God that, unlike Yahweh, coincides with the epitome of good.
It would have been very different if the John of the Epistles
had been obliged to discuss these matters with the John of
Revelation. Later generations could afford to ignore the dark
side of the Apocalypse, because the specifically Christian
achievement was something that was not to be frivolously endangered. But for modern man the case is quite otherwise. We
have experienced things so unheard of and so staggering that
the question of whether such things are in any way reconcilable
with the idea of a good God has become burningly topical. It
is no longer a problem for experts in theological seminaries,
but a universal religious nightmare, to the solution of which
even a layman in theology like myself can, or perhaps must,
make a contribution.

737 I have tried to set forth above the inescapable conclusions
which must, I believe, be reached if one looks at tradition
with critical common sense. If, in this wise, one is confronted
with a paradoxical idea of God, and if, as a religious person,
one considers at the same time the full extent of the problem,
one finds oneself in the situation of the author of Revelation,
who we may suppose was a convinced Christian. His possible
identity with the writer of the letters brings out the acuteness
of the contradiction: What is the relationship of this man to
God? How does he endure the intolerable contradiction in the
nature of Deity? Although we know nothing of his conscious
decision, we believe we may find some clue in the vision of the
sun-woman in travail.

738 The paradoxical nature of God has a like effect on man: it
tears him asunder into opposites and delivers him over to a
seemingly insoluble conflict. What happens in such a condition?
Here we must let psychology speak, for psychology represents the
sum of all the observations and insights it has gained from the
empirical study of severe states of conflict. There are, for

example, conflicts of duty no one knows how to solve. Consciousness only knows: *tertium non datur!* The doctor therefore advises his patient to wait and see whether the unconscious will not produce a dream which proposes an irrational and therefore unexpected third thing as a solution. As experience shows, symbols of a reconciling and unitive nature do in fact turn up in dreams, the most frequent being the motif of the child-hero and the squaring of the circle, signifying the union of opposites. Those who have no access to these specifically medical experiences can derive practical instruction from fairy tales, and particularly from alchemy. The real subject of Hermetic philosophy is the *coniunctio oppositorum*. Alchemy characterizes its "child" on the one hand as the stone (e.g., the carbuncle), and on the other hand as the homunculus, or the *filius sapientiae* or even the *homo altus*. This is precisely the figure we meet in the Apocalypse as the son of the sun-woman, whose birth story seems like a paraphrase of the birth of Christ—a paraphrase which was repeated in various forms by the alchemists. In fact, they posit their stone as a parallel to Christ (this, with one exception, without reference to the Book of Revelation). This motif appears again in corresponding form and in corresponding situations in the dreams of modern man, with no connection with alchemy, and always it has to do with the bringing together of the light and the dark, as though modern man, like the alchemists, had divined what the problem was that the Apocalypse set the future. It was this problem on which the alchemists laboured for nearly seventeen centuries, and it is the same problem that distresses modern man. Though in one respect he knows more, in another respect he knows less than the alchemists. The problem for him is no longer projected upon matter, as it was for them; but on the other hand it has become psychologically acute, so that the psychotherapist has more to say on these matters than the theologian, who has remained caught in his archaic figures of speech. The doctor, often very much against his will, is forced by the problems of psychoneurosis to look more closely at the religious problem. It is not without good reason that I myself have reached the age of seventy-six before venturing to catechize myself as to the nature of those "ruling ideas" which decide our ethical behaviour and have such an important influence on our practical life. They are in the last resort the principles which, spoken or unspoken, determine the moral decisions upon which our existence depends, for weal or woe. All these dominants culminate in the positive or negative concept of God.[1]

739 Ever since John the apocalyptist experienced for the first time (perhaps unconsciously) the conflict into which Christianity inevitably leads, mankind has groaned under this burden: *God wanted to become man, and still wants to.* That is probably why John experienced in his vision a second birth of a son from the mother Sophia, a divine birth which was characterized by a *coniunctio oppositorum* and which anticipated the *filius sapientiae*, the essence of the individuation process. This was the effect of Christianity on a Christian of early times, who had lived long and resolutely enough to be able to cast a glance into the distant future. The mediation between the opposites was already indicated in the symbolism of Christ's fate, in the crucifixion scene where the mediator hangs between two thieves, one of whom goes to paradise, the other down to hell. Inevitably, in the Christian view, the opposition had to lie between God and man, and man was always in danger of being identified with the dark side. This, and the predestinarian hints dropped by our Lord, influenced John strongly: only the few preordained from eternity shall be saved, while the great mass of mankind shall perish in the final catastrophe. The opposition between God and man in the Christian view may well be a Yahwistic legacy from olden times, when the metaphysical problem consisted solely in Yahweh's relations with his people. The fear of Yahweh was still too great for anybody to dare—despite Job's gnosis—to lodge the antinomy in Deity itself. But if you keep the opposition between God and man, then you finally arrive, whether you like it or not, at the Christian conclusion "omne bonum a Deo, omne malum ab homine," with the absurd result that the creature is placed in opposition to its creator and a positively cosmic or daemonic grandeur in evil is imputed to man. The terrible destructive will that breaks out in John's ecstasies gives some idea of what it means when man is placed in opposition to the God of goodness: it burdens him with the dark side of God, which in Job is still in its right place. But

---

[1] Psychologically the God-concept includes every idea of the ultimate, of the first or last, of the highest or lowest. The name makes no difference.

93

either way man is identified with evil, with the result that he sets his face against goodness or else tries to be as perfect as his father in heaven.

740   Yahweh's decision to become man is a symbol of the development that had to supervene when man becomes conscious of the sort of God-image he is confronted with.[2] God acts out of the unconscious of man and forces him to harmonize and unite the opposing influences to which his mind is exposed from the unconscious. The unconscious wants both: to divide and to unite. In his striving for unity, therefore, man may always count on the help of a metaphysical advocate, as Job clearly recognized. The unconscious wants to flow into consciousness in order to reach the light, but at the same time it continually thwarts itself, because it would rather remain unconscious. That is to say, God wants to become man, but not quite. The conflict in his nature is so great that the incarnation can only be bought by an expiatory self-sacrifice offered up to the wrath of God's dark side.

741   At first, God incarnated his good side in order, as we may suppose, to create the most durable basis for a later assimilation of the other side. From the promise of the Paraclete we may conclude that God wants to become *wholly* man; in other words, to reproduce himself in his own dark creature (man not redeemed from original sin). The author of Revelation has left us a testimony to the continued operation of the Holy Ghost in the sense of a continuing incarnation. He was a creaturely man who was invaded by the dark God of wrath and vengeance—a *ventus urens,* a 'burning wind.' (This John was possibly the favourite disciple, who in old age was vouchsafed a premonition of future developments.) This disturbing invasion engendered in him the image of the divine child, of a future saviour, born of the divine consort whose reflection (the anima) lives in every man—that child whom Meister Eckhart also saw in a vision. It was he who knew that God alone in his Godhead is not in a state of bliss, but must be born in the human soul ("Gott ist selig

2 The God-concept, as the idea of an all-embracing totality, also includes the unconscious, and hence, in contrast to consciousness, it includes the objective psyche, which so often frustrates the will and intentions of the conscious mind. Prayer, for instance, reinforces the potential of the unconscious, thus accounting for the sometimes unexpected effects of prayer.

in der Seele"). The incarnation in Christ is the prototype which is continually being transferred to the creature by the Holy Ghost.

742   Since our moral conduct can hardly be compared with that of an early Christian like John, all manner of good as well as evil can still break through in us, particularly in regard to love. A sheer will for destruction, such as was evident in John, is not to be expected in our case. In all my experience I have never observed anything like it, except in cases of severe psychoses and criminal insanity. As a result of the spiritual differentiation fostered by the Reformation, and by the growth of the sciences in particular (which were originally taught by the fallen angels), there is already a considerable admixture of darkness in us, so that, compared with the purity of the early Christian saints (and some of the later ones too), we do not show up in a very favourable light. Our comparative blackness naturally does not help us a bit. Though it mitigates the impact of evil forces, it makes us more vulnerable and less capable of resisting them. We therefore need more light, more goodness and moral strength, and must wash off as much of the obnoxious blackness as possible, otherwise we shall not be able to assimilate the dark God who also wants to become man, and at the same time endure him without perishing. For this all the Christian virtues are needed and something else besides, for the problem is not only moral: we also need the Wisdom that Job was seeking. But at that time she was still hidden in Yahweh, or rather, she was not yet remembered by him. That higher and "complete" ($\tau \acute{\epsilon} \lambda \epsilon \iota o s$) man is begotten by the "unknown" father and born from Wisdom, and it is he who, in the figure of the *puer aeternus*—"vultu mutabilis albus et ater" [3]—represents our totality, which transcends consciousness. It was this boy into whom Faust had to change, abandoning his inflated onesidedness which saw the devil only outside. Christ's "Except ye become as little children" prefigures this change, for in them the opposites lie close together; but what is meant is the boy who is born from the maturity of the adult man, and not the unconscious child we would like to remain. Looking ahead, Christ also hinted, as I mentioned before, at a morality of evil.

743   Strangely, suddenly, as if it did not belong there, the sun-

3 "Of changeful countenance, both white and black." Horace, *Epistulae,* II, 2.

woman with her child appears in the stream of apocalyptic visions. He belongs to another, future world. Hence, like the Jewish Messiah, the child is "caught up" to God, and his mother must stay for a long time hidden in the wilderness, where she is nourished by God. For the immediate and urgent problem in those days was not the union of opposites, which lay in the future, but the incarnation of the light and the good, the subjugation of *concupiscentia,* the lust of this world, and the consolidation of the *civitas Dei* against the advent of the Antichrist, who would come after a thousand years to announce the horrors of the last days, the epiphany of the wrathful and avenging God. The Lamb, transformed into a demonic ram, reveals a new gospel, the *Evangelium Aeternum,* which, going right beyond the love of God, has the fear of God as its main ingredient. Therefore the Apocalypse closes, like the classical individuation process, with the symbol of the *hieros gamos,* the marriage of the son with the mother-bride. But the marriage takes place in heaven, where "nothing unclean" enters, high above the devastated world. Light consorts with light. That is the programme for the Christian aeon which must be fulfilled before God can incarnate in the creaturely man. Only in the last days will the vision of the sun-woman be fulfilled. In recognition of this truth, and evidently inspired by the workings of the Holy Ghost, the Pope has recently announced the dogma of the *Assumptio Mariae,* very much to the astonishment of all rationalists. Mary as the bride is united with the son in the heavenly bridal-chamber, and, as Sophia, with the Godhead.[4]

744   This dogma is in every respect timely. In the first place it is a symbolical fulfilment of John's vision.[5] Secondly, it con-

4 *Apostolic Constitution* ("*Munificentissimus Deus*") *of . . . Pius XII,* §22: "Oportebat sponsam, quam Pater desponsaverat, in thalamis caelestibus habitare" (The place of the bride whom the Father had espoused was in the heavenly courts).—St. John Damascene, *Encomium in Dormitionem, etc.,* Homily II, 14 (cf. Migne, *P.G.,* vol. 96, col. 742). §30: Comparison with the Bride in the Song of Solomon. §33: ". . . ita pariter surrexit et Arca sanctificationis suae, cum in hac die Virgo Mater ad aethereum thalamum est assumpta" (. . . so in like manner arose the Ark which he had sanctified, when on this day the Virgin Mother was taken up to her heavenly bridal-chamber).—St. Anthony of Padua, *Sermones Dominicales, etc.* (ed. Locatelli, III, p. 730).

5 *Apostolic Constitution,* §31: "Ac praeterea scholastici doctores non modo in variis Veteris Testamenti figuris, sed in illa etiam Muliere amicta sole, quam Joannes Apostolus in insula Patmo [Rev. 12 : 1ff.] contemplatus est, Assumptionem

tains an allusion to the marriage of the Lamb at the end of time, and, thirdly, it repeats the Old Testament anamnesis of Sophia. These three references foretell the Incarnation of God. The second and third foretell the Incarnation in Christ,[6] but the first foretells the Incarnation in creaturely man.

XVIII

745   Everything now depends on man: immense power of destruction is given into his hand, and the question is whether he can resist the will to use it, and can temper his will with the spirit of love and wisdom. He will hardly be capable of doing so on his own unaided resources. He needs the help of an "advocate" in heaven, that is, of the child who was caught up to God and who brings the "healing" and making whole of the hitherto fragmentary man. Whatever man's wholeness, or the self, may mean *per se,* empirically it is an image of the goal of life spontaneously produced by the unconscious, irrespective of the wishes and fears of the conscious mind. It stands for the goal of the total man, for the realization of his wholeness and individuality with or without the consent of his will. The dynamic of this process is instinct, which ensures that everything which belongs to an individual's life shall enter into it, whether he consents or not, or is conscious of what is happening to him or not. Obviously, it makes a great deal of difference subjectively whether he knows what he is living out, whether he understands what he is doing, and whether he accepts responsibility for what he proposes to do or has done. The difference between conscious realization and the lack of it has been roundly formulated in the saying of Christ already quoted: "Man, if indeed thou knowest what thou doest, thou art blessed: but if thou knowest not, thou art cursed, and a transgressor of the law." [1] Before the bar of

---

Deiparae Virginis significatam viderunt" (Moreover, the Scholastic doctors saw the Assumption of the Virgin Mother of God signified not only in the various figures of the Old Testament, but also in the Woman clothed with the sun, whom the Apostle John contemplated on the island of Patmos).

6 The marriage of the Lamb repeats the Annunciation and the Overshadowing of Mary.

1 Codex Bezae, apocryphal insertion at Luke 6:4. [Trans. by James; see above, par. 696, n. 6.—TRANS.]

nature and fate, unconsciousness is never accepted as an excuse; on the contrary there are very severe penalties for it. Hence all unconscious nature longs for the light of consciousness while frantically struggling against it at the same time.

746   The conscious realization of what is hidden and kept secret certainly confronts us with an insoluble conflict; at least this is how it appears to the conscious mind. But the symbols that rise up out of the unconscious in dreams show it rather as a confrontation of opposites, and the images of the goal represent their successful reconciliation. Something empirically demonstrable comes to our aid from the depths of our unconscious nature. It is the task of the conscious mind to understand these hints. If this does not happen, the process of individuation will nevertheless continue. The only difference is that we become its victims and are dragged along by fate towards that inescapable goal which we might have reached walking upright, if only we had taken the trouble and been patient enough to understand in time the meaning of the numina that cross our path. The only thing that really matters now is whether man can climb up to a higher moral level, to a higher plane of consciousness, in order to be equal to the superhuman powers which the fallen angels have played into his hands. But he can make no progress with himself unless he becomes very much better acquainted with his own nature. Unfortunately, a terrifying ignorance prevails in this respect, and an equally great aversion to increasing the knowledge of his intrinsic character. However, in the most unexpected quarters nowadays we find people who can no longer blink the fact that something *ought* to be done with man in regard to his psychology. Unfortunately, the little word "ought" tells us that they do not know what to do, and do not know the way that leads to the goal. We can, of course, hope for the undeserved grace of God, who hears our prayers. But God, who also does *not* hear our prayers, wants to become man, and for that purpose he has chosen, through the Holy Ghost, the creaturely man filled with darkness—the natural man who is tainted with original sin and who learnt the divine arts and sciences from the fallen angels. The guilty man is eminently suitable and is therefore chosen to become the vessel for the continuing incarnation, not the guiltless one who holds aloof

from the world and refuses to pay his tribute to life, for in him the dark God would find no room.

747   Since the Apocalypse we now know again that God is not only to be loved, but also to be feared. He fills us with evil as well as with good, otherwise he would not need to be feared; and because he wants to become man, the uniting of his antinomy must take place in man. This involves man in a new responsibility. He can no longer wriggle out of it on the plea of his littleness and nothingness, for the dark God has slipped the atom bomb and chemical weapons into his hands and given him the power to empty out the apocalyptic vials of wrath on his fellow creatures. Since he has been granted an almost godlike power, he can no longer remain blind and unconscious. He must know something of God's nature and of metaphysical processes if he is to understand himself and thereby achieve gnosis of the Divine.

XIX

748   The promulgation of the new dogma of the Assumption of the Virgin Mary could, in itself, have been sufficient reason for examining the psychological background. It was interesting to note that, among the many articles published in the Catholic and Protestant press on the declaration of the dogma, there was not one, so far as I could see, which laid anything like the proper emphasis on what was undoubtedly the most powerful motive: namely, the popular movement and the psychological need behind it. Essentially, the writers of the articles were satisfied with learned considerations, dogmatic and historical, which have no bearing on the living religious process. But anyone who has followed with attention the visions of Mary which have been increasing in number over the last few decades, and has taken their psychological significance into account, might have known what was brewing. The fact, especially, that it was largely children who had the visions might have given pause for thought, for in such cases the collective unconscious is always at work. Incidentally, the Pope himself is rumoured to have had several visions of the Mother of God on the occasion of the declaration. One could have known for a long time that there was a deep

longing in the masses for an intercessor and mediatrix who would at last take her place alongside the Holy Trinity and be received as the "Queen of Heaven and Bride at the heavenly court." For more than a thousand years it had been taken for granted that the Mother of God dwelt there, and we know from the Old Testament that Sophia was with God before the creation. From the ancient Egyptian theology of the divine Pharaohs we know that God wants to become man by means of a human mother, and it was recognized even in prehistoric times that the primordial divine being is both male and female. But such a truth eventuates in time only when it is solemnly proclaimed or rediscovered. It is psychologically significant for our day that in the year 1950 the heavenly bride was united with the bridegroom. In order to interpret this event, one has to consider not only the arguments adduced by the Papal Bull, but the prefigurations in the apocalyptic marriage of the Lamb and in the Old Testament anamnesis of Sophia. The nuptial union in the *thalamus* (bridal-chamber) signifies the *hieros gamos,* and this in turn is the first step towards incarnation, towards the birth of the saviour who, since antiquity, was thought of as the *filius solis et lunae,* the *filius sapientiae,* and the equivalent of Christ. When, therefore, a longing for the exaltation of the Mother of God passes through the people, this tendency, if thought to its logical conclusion, means the desire for the birth of a saviour, a peacemaker, a "mediator pacem faciens inter inimicos." [1] Although he is already born in the pleroma, his birth in time can only be accomplished when it is perceived, recognized, and declared by man.

749   The motive and content of the popular movement which contributed to the Pope's decision solemnly to declare the new dogma consist not in the birth of a new god, but in the continuing incarnation of God which began with Christ. Arguments based on historical criticism will never do justice to the new dogma; on the contrary, they are as lamentably wide of the mark as are the unqualified fears to which the English archbishops have given expression. In the first place, the declaration of the dogma has changed nothing in principle in the Catholic ideology as it has existed for more than a thousand years; and in the second place, the failure to understand that God has

[1] "A mediator making peace between enemies."

eternally wanted to become man, and for that purpose continually incarnates through the Holy Ghost in the temporal sphere, is an alarming symptom and can only mean that the Protestant standpoint has lost ground by not understanding the signs of the times and by ignoring the continued operation of the Holy Ghost. It is obviously out of touch with the tremendous archetypal happenings in the psyche of the individual and the masses, and with the symbols which are intended to compensate the truly apocalyptic world situation today.[2] It seems to have succumbed to a species of rationalistic historicism and to have lost any understanding of the Holy Ghost who works in the hidden places of the soul. It can therefore neither understand nor admit a further revelation of the divine drama.

750   This circumstance has given me, a layman in things theological, cause to put forward my views on these dark matters. My attempt is based on the psychological experience I have harvested during the course of a long life. I do not underestimate the psyche in any respect whatsoever, nor do I imagine for a moment that psychic happenings vanish into thin air by being explained. Psychologism represents a still primitive mode of magical thinking, with the help of which one hopes to conjure the reality of the soul out of existence, after the manner of the "Proktophantasmist" in *Faust:*

> Are you still here? Nay, it's a thing unheard.
> Vanish at once! We've said the enlightening word.

751   One would be very ill advised to identify me with such a childish standpoint. However, I have been asked so often whether I believe in the existence of God or not that I am somewhat concerned lest I be taken for an adherent of "psychologism" far more commonly than I suspect. What most

---

[2] The papal rejection of psychological symbolism may be explained by the fact that the Pope is primarily concerned with the reality of metaphysical happenings. Owing to the undervaluation of the psyche that everywhere prevails, every attempt at adequate psychological understanding is immediately suspected of psychologism. It is understandable that dogma must be protected from this danger. If, in physics, one seeks to explain the nature of light, nobody expects that as a result there will be no light. But in the case of psychology everybody believes that what it explains is explained away. However, I cannot expect that my particular deviationist point of view could be known in any competent quarter.

people overlook or seem unable to understand is the fact that I regard the psyche as *real*. They believe only in physical facts, and must consequently come to the conclusion that either the uranium itself or the laboratory equipment created the atom bomb. That is no less absurd than the assumption that a non-real psyche is responsible for it. God is an obvious psychic and non-physical fact, i.e., a fact that can be established psychically but not physically. Equally, these people have still not got it into their heads that the psychology of religion falls into two categories, which must be sharply distinguished from one another: firstly, the psychology of the religious person, and secondly, the psychology of religion proper, i.e., of religious contents.

752   It is chiefly my experiences in the latter field which have given me the courage to enter into the discussion of the religious question and especially into the pros and cons of the dogma of the Assumption—which, by the way, I consider to be the most important religious event since the Reformation. It is a *petra scandali* for the unpsychological mind: how can such an unfounded assertion as the bodily reception of the Virgin into heaven be put forward as worthy of belief? But the method which the Pope uses in order to demonstrate the truth of the dogma makes sense to the psychological mind, because it bases itself firstly on the necessary prefigurations, and secondly on a tradition of religious assertions reaching back for more than a thousand years. Clearly, the material evidence for the existence of this psychic phenomenon is more than sufficient. It does not matter at all that a physically impossible fact is asserted, because all religious assertions are physical impossibilities. If they were not so, they would, as I said earlier, necessarily be treated in the text-books of natural science. But religious statements without exception have to do with the reality of the *psyche* and not with the reality of *physis*. What outrages the Protestant standpoint in particular is the boundless approximation of the Deipara to the Godhead and, in consequence, the endangered supremacy of Christ, from which Protestantism will not budge. In sticking to this point it has obviously failed to consider that its hymnology is full of references to the "heavenly bridegroom," who is now suddenly supposed not to have a bride with equal rights. Or has, perchance, the "bridegroom," in true psychologistic manner, been understood as a mere metaphor?

753   The logical consistency of the papal declaration cannot be surpassed, and it leaves Protestantism with the odium of being nothing but a *man's religion* which allows no metaphysical representation of woman. In this respect it is similar to Mithraism, and Mithraism found this prejudice very much to its detriment. Protestantism has obviously not given sufficient attention to the signs of the times which point to the equality of women. But this equality requires to be metaphysically anchored in the figure of a "divine" woman, the bride of Christ. Just as the person of Christ cannot be replaced by an organization, so the bride cannot be replaced by the Church. The feminine, like the masculine, demands an equally personal representation.

754   The dogmatizing of the Assumption does not, however, according to the dogmatic view, mean that Mary has attained the status of a goddess, although, as mistress of heaven (as opposed to the prince of the sublunary aerial realm, Satan) and mediatrix, she is functionally on a par with Christ, the king and mediator. At any rate her position satisfies the need of the archetype. The new dogma expresses a renewed hope for the fulfilment of that yearning for peace which stirs deep down in the soul, and for a resolution of the threatening tension between the opposites. Everyone shares this tension and everyone experiences it in his individual form of unrest, the more so the less he sees any possibility of getting rid of it by rational means. It is no wonder, therefore, that the hope, indeed the expectation of divine intervention arises in the collective unconscious and at the same time in the masses. The papal declaration has given comforting expression to this yearning. How could Protestantism so completely miss the point? This lack of understanding can only be explained by the fact that the dogmatic symbols and hermeneutic allegories have lost their meaning for Protestant rationalism. This is also true, in some measure, of the opposition to the new dogma within the Catholic Church itself, or rather to the dogmatization of the old doctrine. Naturally, a certain degree of rationalism is better suited to Protestantism than it is to the Catholic outlook. The latter gives the archetypal symbolisms the necessary freedom and space in which to develop over the centuries while at the same time insisting on their original form, unperturbed by intellectual difficulties and the objections of rationalists. In this way the Catholic Church

demonstrates her maternal character, because she allows the tree growing out of her matrix to develop according to its own laws. Protestantism, in contrast, is committed to the paternal spirit. Not only did it develop, at the outset, from an encounter with the worldly spirit of the times, but it continues this dialectic with the spiritual currents of every age; for the pneuma, in keeping with its original wind nature, is flexible, ever in living motion, comparable now to water, now to fire. It can desert its original haunts, can even go astray and get lost, if it succumbs too much to the spirit of the age. In order to fulfil its task, the Protestant spirit must be full of unrest and occasionally troublesome; it must even be revolutionary, so as to make sure that tradition has an influence on the change of contemporary values. The shocks it sustains during this encounter modify and at the same time enliven the tradition, which in its slow progress through the centuries would, without these disturbances, finally arrive at complete petrifaction and thus lose its effect. By merely criticizing and opposing certain developments within the Catholic Church, Protestantism would gain only a miserable bit of vitality, unless, mindful of the fact that Christianity consists of two separate camps, or rather, is a disunited brother-sister pair, it remembers that besides defending its own existence it must acknowledge Catholicism's right to exist too. A brother who for theological reasons wanted to cut the thread of his elder sister's life would rightly be called inhuman—to say nothing of Christian charity—and the converse is also true. Nothing is achieved by merely negative criticism. It is justified only to the degree that it is creative. Therefore it would seem profitable to me if, for example, Protestantism admitted that it is shocked by the new dogma not only because it throws a distressing light on the gulf between brother and sister, but because, for fundamental reasons, a situation has developed within Christianity which removes it further than ever from the sphere of worldly understanding. Protestantism knows, or could know, how much it owes its very existence to the Catholic Church. How much or how little does the Protestant still possess if he can no longer criticize or protest? In view of the intellectual *skandalon* which the new dogma represents, he should remind himself of his Christian responsibility—"Am I my brother's (or in this case, my sister's) keeper?"—and examine in all seriousness the reasons, explicit or otherwise, that decided the declaration of the new dogma. In so doing, he should guard against casting cheap aspersions and would do well to assume that there is more in it than papal arbitrariness. It would be desirable for the Protestant to understand that the new dogma has placed upon him a new responsibility toward the worldly spirit of our age, for he cannot simply deny his problematical sister before the eyes of the world. He must, even if he finds her antipathetic, be fair to her if he does not want to lose his self-respect. For instance, this is a favourable opportunity for him to ask himself, for a change, what is the meaning not only of the new dogma but of all more or less dogmatic assertions over and above their literal concretism. Considering the arbitrary and protean state of his own dogmas, and the precarious, schism-riven condition of his Church, he cannot afford to remain rigid and impervious to the spirit of the age. And since, in accordance with his obligations to the *Zeitgeist*, he is more concerned to come to terms with the world and its ideas than with God, it would seem clearly indicated that, on the occasion of the entry of the Mother of God into the heavenly bridal-chamber, he should bend to the great task of reinterpreting all the Christian traditions. If it is a question of truths which are anchored deep in the soul—and no one with the slightest insight can doubt this fact—then the solution of this task must be possible. For this we need the freedom of the spirit, which, as we know, is assured only in Protestantism. The dogma of the Assumption is a slap in the face for the historical and rationalistic view of the world, and would remain so for all time if one were to insist obstinately on the arguments of reason and history. This is a case, if ever there was one, where psychological understanding is needed, because the mythologem coming to light is so obvious that we must be deliberately blinding ourselves if we cannot see its symbolic nature and interpret it in symbolic terms.

755   The dogmatization of the *Assumptio Mariae* points to the *hieros gamos* in the pleroma, and this in turn implies, as we have said, the future birth of the divine child, who, in accordance with the divine trend towards incarnation, will choose as his birthplace the empirical man. The metaphysical process is known to the psychology of the unconscious as the individuation process. In so far as this process, as a rule, runs its course un-

unconsciously as it has from time immemorial, it means no more than that the acorn becomes an oak, the calf a cow, and the child an adult. But if the individuation process is made conscious, consciousness must confront the unconscious and a balance between the opposites must be found. As this is not possible through logic, one is dependent on *symbols* which make the irrational union of opposites possible. They are produced spontaneously by the unconscious and are amplified by the conscious mind. The central symbols of this process describe the self, which is man's totality, consisting on the one hand of that which is conscious to him, and on the other hand of the contents of the unconscious. The self is the τέλειος ἄνθρωπος, the whole man, whose symbols are the divine child and its synonyms. This is only a very summary sketch of the process, but it can be observed at any time in modern man, or one can read about it in the documents of Hermetic philosophy from the Middle Ages. The parallelism between the symbols is astonishing to anyone who knows both the psychology of the unconscious and alchemy.

756   The difference between the "natural" individuation process, which runs its course unconsciously, and the one which is consciously realized, is tremendous. In the first case consciousness nowhere intervenes; the end remains as dark as the beginning. In the second case so much darkness comes to light that the personality is permeated with light, and consciousness necessarily gains in scope and insight. The encounter between conscious and unconscious has to ensure that the light which shines in the darkness is not only comprehended by the darkness, but comprehends it. The *filius solis et lunae* is the symbol of the union of opposites as well as the catalyst of their union. It is the alpha and omega of the process, the mediator and intermedius. "It has a thousand names," say the alchemists, meaning that the source from which the individuation process rises and the goal towards which it aims is nameless, ineffable.

757   It is only through the psyche that we can establish that God acts upon us, but we are unable to distinguish whether these actions emanate from God or from the unconscious. We cannot tell whether God and the unconscious are two different entities. Both are border-line concepts for transcendental contents. But empirically it can be established, with a sufficient degree of probability, that there is in the unconscious an archetype of

wholeness which manifests itself spontaneously in dreams, etc., and a tendency, independent of the conscious will, to relate other archetypes to this centre. Consequently, it does not seem improbable that the archetype of wholeness occupies as such a central position which approximates it to the God-image. The similarity is further borne out by the peculiar fact that the archetype produces a symbolism which has always characterized and expressed the Deity. These facts make possible a certain qualification of our above thesis concerning the indistinguishableness of God and the unconscious. Strictly speaking, the God-image does not coincide with the unconscious as such, but with a special content of it, namely the archetype of the self. It is this archetype from which we can no longer distinguish the God-image empirically. We can arbitrarily postulate a difference between these two entities, but that does not help us at all. On the contrary, it only helps us to separate man from God, and prevents God from becoming man. Faith is certainly right when it impresses on man's mind and heart how infinitely far away and inaccessible God is; but it also teaches his nearness, his immediate presence, and it is just this nearness which has to be empirically real if it is not to lose all significance. Only that which acts upon me do I recognize as real and actual. But that which has no effect upon me might as well not exist. The religious need longs for wholeness, and therefore lays hold of the images of wholeness offered by the unconscious, which, independently of the conscious mind, rise up from the depths of our psychic nature.

XX

758   It will probably have become clear to the reader that the account I have given of the development of symbolic entities corresponds to a process of differentiation of human consciousness. But since, as I showed in the introduction, the archetypes in question are not mere objects of the mind, but are also autonomous factors, i.e., living subjects, the differentiation of consciousness can be understood as the effect of the intervention of transcendentally conditioned dynamisms. In this case it would be the archetypes that accomplish the primary transformation.

But since, in our experience, there are no psychic conditions which could be observed *through introspection* outside the human being, the behaviour of the archetypes cannot be investigated at all without the interaction of the observing consciousness. Therefore the question as to whether the process is initiated by consciousness or by the archetype can never be answered; unless, in contradiction to experience, one either robbed the archetype of its autonomy or degraded consciousness to a mere machine. We find ourselves in best agreement with psychological experience if we concede to the archetype a definite measure of independence, and to consciousness a degree of creative freedom proportionate to its scope. There then arises that reciprocal action between two relatively autonomous factors which compels us, when describing and explaining the processes, to present sometimes the one and sometimes the other factor as the acting subject, even when God becomes man. The Christian solution has hitherto avoided this difficulty by recognizing Christ as the one and only God-man. But the indwelling of the Holy Ghost, the third Divine Person, in man, brings about a Christification of many, and the question then arises whether these many are all complete God-men. Such a transformation would lead to insufferable collisions between them, to say nothing of the unavoidable inflation to which the ordinary mortal, who is not freed from original sin, would instantly succumb. In these circumstances it is well to remind ourselves of St. Paul and his split consciousness: on one side he felt he was the apostle directly called and enlightened by God, and, on the other side, a sinful man who could not pluck out the "thorn in the flesh" and rid himself of the Satanic angel who plagued him. That is to say, even the enlightened person remains what he is, and is never more than his own limited ego before the One who dwells within him, whose form has no knowable boundaries, who encompasses him on all sides, fathomless as the abysms of the earth and vast as the sky.

BIBLIOGRAPHY

ANTHONY OF PADUA, SAINT. *S. Antonii Patavini Sermones dominicales et in solemnitatibus.* Edited by Antonio Maria Locatelli. Padua, 1895. 3 vols.

CHARLES, ROBERT HENRY (ed.). *The Apocrypha and Pseudepigrapha of the Old Testament in English.* Oxford, 1913. 2 vols.

FRANZ, MARIE-LOUISE VON. *Die Passio Perpetuae.* In: C. G. JUNG. *Aion: Untersuchungen zur Symbolgeschichte.* Zurich, 1951.

JAMES, MONTAGUE RHODES (trans.). *The Apocryphal New Testament.* Oxford, 1924.

JUNG, CARL GUSTAV. *Aion: Researches into the Phenomenology of the Self. Collected Works,* * Vol. 9, part ii.

———. "On the Nature of the Psyche." In: *Collected Works,* Vol. 8.

———. "Psychological Commentary on 'The Tibetan Book of the Dead'." In: *Collected Works,* Vol. 11.

———. "Transformation Symbolism in the Mass." In: *Collected Works,* Vol. 11.

MIGNE, JACQUES PAUL (ed.). *Patrologiae cursus completus.*
[*P.L.*] Latin Series. Paris, 1844–64. 221 vols.
[*P.G.*] Greek Series. Paris, 1857–66. 166 vols.
(These works are referred to in the text and in this bibliography as "Migne, *P.L.*" and "Migne, *P.G.*" respectively. References are to columns, not to pages.)

SCHOLEM, GERSHOM G. *Major Trends in Jewish Mysticism.* New York, 1941; 3rd edn., 1954.

TERTULLIAN. *Adversus Judaeos.* In Migne, *P.L.*, vol. 2, cols. 595-642. For translation, see: *The Writings of Tertullianus.* Translated by S. Thelwall, P. Holmes, and others. Vol. III. (Ante-Nicene Christian Library, 18.) Edinburgh, 1870.

* For details of the *Collected Works of C. G. Jung,* see the list at the end of this volume.

INDEX

In entries relating to the books of the Bible, the numbers in parentheses indicate the chapter and verse(s) referred to.

Paraclete *(cont.)*
truth, 51, 69, 71; as Wisdom, 27; work in individuals, 71; *see also* Christ; Holy Ghost
parthenoi, 83
Paul, St., 71, 73; epistles of, 45, *see also under names of specific epistles*; identified with Hermes, 52; split consciousness of, 108
Pegasus, 84*n*
peregrinatio, 62
perfection: of Christ, 37; as masculine, 33; symbol of, 85
perfectionism, 33, 37
Pergamum, 74
peripeteia, 44
Perpetua, St., 80
Persian: mythology, 13*n*
Peter, St., 72
Phanuel, 64, 69
Philadelphia, 74
philosophers' stone, parallel of Christ, 72; tetrameria of, 86
philosophy, Indian, 79; natural, medieval, x
physician, *see* doctor
Physis, 102
Pisces: aeon of, 84, 85, 88; sign of, 44; *see also* Fishes
Pius XII, Pope, 96*n*, 99*f*
pleroma/pleromatic, 32, 38, 62, 63, 89, 100; Bardo State, 32; Ezekiel as son of man in, 66; *hieros gamos* in, 35, 105; pre-existence of Yahweh and Sophia in, 85*f*
pneuma (πνεῦμα), antimimon, 50; circle as symbol of, 85; flexibility of, 104; *hagion*, 45; *see also* Holy Ghost; pneumatic nature of quaternity, 62; Sophia as, 24, 26, 31; *see also* Nous
pope, *see* Pius XII
prayer, 94*n*
predestination, 45, 83, 93
prima materia, 39; Adam produced from, 29
primitive(s): and religion, xiii

"Prince of this world," *see* "Lord of this world"
privatio boni, ix, 21*n*, 66
Protestantism, on dogma of Assumption, 100*ff*; and Holy Ghost, 101; a man's religion, 103; on revelation, 51; revolutionary role, 104
Proverbs (book), 24; (8 : 22–31), 24*f*; (8 : 29*f*), 41
Psalms (book), 12; (82 : 6), 70; (89), 10, 12, 56, 66; (89: 28, 34, 35), 8; (89 : 46, 47, 49), 9
psyche, autonomous, xii; reality of, 102
psychologism, xiv, 101
psychology: and dogma of Assumption, 99*ff*; empirical, 46*f*; and nature of God, 91*ff*; of religion, two categories, 102
psychoneuroses, 92
psychopathology, and religion, 92; visions and, 58
psychotherapy, and conflicts of duty, 92; and hostile brothers motif, 38
puer aeternus, 95; *see also* divine child
Purusha, purusha-atman doctrine, 59, 79

Q

quaternarium, see quaternity
quaternio, 61
quaternity, 85*f*; in alchemy, 61; divine, 63; in Ezekiel and Enoch, 58*f*, 61*ff*; Hades of Enoch as, 61; pleromatic split in, 62; pneumatic nature of, 61; of Son of Man, 68; symbols of, 68, 75

R

rainbow, sign of contract, 12
ram, 75, 96
Raphael, 64

PRINCETON / BOLLINGEN PAPERBACK EDITIONS

FROM THE COLLECTED WORKS OF C. G. JUNG

Aion (CW 9,ii)
Alchemical Studies (CW 13)
Archetypes of the Collective Unconscious (CW 9,i)
Aspects of the Feminine
Aspects of the Masculine
Basic Writings of C. G. Jung
The Development of Personality (CW 17)
Dreams
Essays on Contemporary Events
Essays on a Science of Mythology
The Essential Jung
Flying Saucers
Four Archetypes
Freud and Psychoanalysis (CW 4)
Mandala Symbolism
On the Nature of the Psyche
The Practice of Psychotherapy (CW 16)
Psyche and Symbol
Psychiatric Studies (CW 1)
Psychogenesis of Mental Disease (CW 3)
Psychological Types (CW 6)
Psychology and Alchemy (CW 12)
Psychology and the East
Psychology and the Occult
Psychology and Western Religion
The Psychology of the Transference
The Spirit in Man, Art, and Literature (CW 15)
Symbols of Transformation (CW 5)
Synchronicity
Two Essays on Analytical Psychology (CW 7)
The Undiscovered Self

OTHER BOLLINGEN PAPERBACKS BY C. G. JUNG

C. G. Jung Speaking
Psychological Reflections
Selected Letters
Word and Image